HUEmongous

the CMYK Designer's Companion

HUEMONGOUS
The CMYK Designer's Companion
by Ashkan Mashhour

ISBN: 978-1-939619-24-2

Cover & interior design, typesetting, artwork, prepress: Ashkan Mashhour

For inquiries, feedback, and suggestions, please contact:
ashkan@cheatsheetmusic.com
For updates, new titles, promotions, and the latest information, visit:
pelemeleworks.com

pelemeleworks.com

CONTENTS

MAP

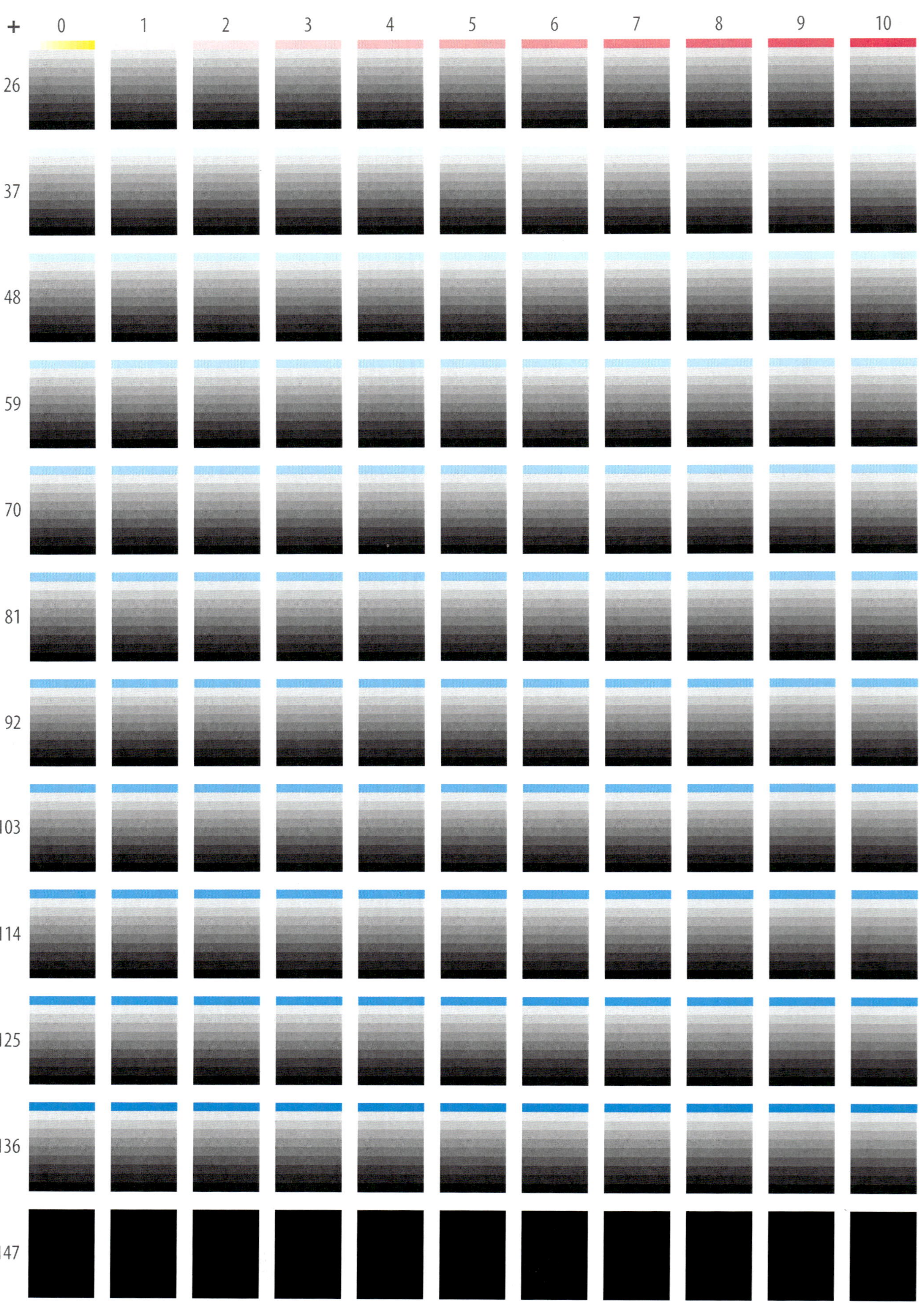

row + column = page number

PREFACE

"The proof is in the pudding" but for designers working with print, "the proof is in the proof"! Sadly, this can bring to light unwelcome discrepancies between the design and the galley, resulting in costly and time-consuming iterations. Colour is notorious for causing many a designer's headaches and experience is the only tool to help mitigate these discrepancies. Experience and aids like this book, that is.

HUEmongous is a colour selection tool—to and from CMYK. A particular use case is to help designers visualise how a solid colour, appearing on their computer monitor, would look like in print. Incorporating *HUEmongous* into your design workflow is simple: select a CMYK colour value in your design software and find the closest match(es) in the book or, select a CMYK swatch in the book and use its value as a starting point in your design software. Beside print production, the book can find applications anytime colour must be quantified or communicated, usually with the goal of being reproduced.

The book comprises two sections. A preliminary section illustrates various aspects of colour and useful characteristics of the CMYK process in hand. The main section presents over 14,000 colour swatches organised in a grid format. Each swatch is formed by combining Cyan (C), Magenta (M), Yellow (Y), and Black (K) inks in various proportions. Ink value is raised in 10 percentage point increments, from 0% to 100%. Colours are ordered in ascending CMYK values (raising K first, then Y, then M, and C last). There is one grid per page, with gradations around the grid. Each grid shows shades of a CMY colour (K from 0 to 90). Blacks (colours with 100K) are grouped together at the end of the section. On manufacturing grounds or to save on ink (and keep costs down), many print shops impose a total ink coverage limit below 400. The visual impact of this limitation on colours is usually quite reasonable and justifies the trade-off. The fifth "colour" to account for is the colour of the paper, which is a flavour of white, though this is typically calibrated out by the printer. Remember to view colours in suitable lighting conditions (e.g., D50).

Throughout the book, CMYK numbers are formatted in percentages (0–100) and are written either in a row or in a column, always in this order: C, M, Y, followed by K. Unless stated otherwise, C/M/Y/K alone refer to ink solids: C (100 0 0 0), M (0 100 0 0), Y (0 0 100 0), K (0 0 0 100). The book is printed in a four-colour CMYK process on coated stock.

CMYK PROCESS SECTION

Using the swatch grids shows by example how to read the colour grids featured in the book.
Tints shows swatches of all four process colours with ink values ranging from 5 to 100 in steps of 5.
Fine step tints shows tints with ink values ranging from 1 to 100, in steps of 1. The value of each swatch is obtained by adding the corresponding label values of the X and Y axes. For example, the swatch value in column 3, row 2, is 20 + 2 = 22.
Gradients presents one- and two-colour gradients. Issues like banding are difficult to predict and gradient smoothness depends on colours involved, length, press, and so forth.
Colour wheel cycles through a palette of colours, gradually mixing in one process colour with another (one or two CMY colours at once, never three, and no K). The colour chart uses the wheel's colours to produce tints and shades for each.
"Shades" of black is a by-product of ink opacity which makes stand-alone black appear more or less washed out on paper. Luckily, other inks can come to the rescue to beef up this greyish black and make it a deeper black with hints of other hues. Several blacks are shown side by side.
Black substitution shows how black ink can stand in for some amounts of CMY inks and reduce total ink coverage.
Overprint demonstrates how an ink seems to show through another ink placed on top of it, altering the perceived colour. Note that the stacking order of elements on a page is unrelated to the order in which the printer lays down inks on paper (e.g., Y first, then M, then C, and K last).
Black overprint showcases the most common ink to overprint. The final row features a K element moving from top to bottom of a stack of C/M/Y elements.
Multiply vs. overprint compares these two print settings that are sometimes mistaken for one another.

The next few pages are not related to colours per se but to the print process and can be useful in the design phase.
Dots shows tiny geometric shapes in all process colours.
Rules shows lines of various widths. The distinction between finer rules may or may not be apparent and is due in part to the press capabilities.
Type shows type of various sizes in all process colours.
Rule and type tints shows that caution should be exercised when combining finely printed elements with screening.
Ink spread highlights how ink can slightly spread on paper, due to factors like ink viscosity or paper absorption. This is also the basis for dot gain. Like misregistration, ink spread can lead to noticeable defects. For example, elements in the design appear narrower on paper or disappear altogether (e.g., serifs in knockout type).

SWATCH GRIDS SECTION

Colour matching is a practical example of matching a colour to swatches in the book.
Separations presents colour plates for all the swatch grids.
Colours features CMYK swatches in grid format.
Blacks features swatches made of any CMY and K = 100.
Swatch shutters are little masks designed to hide swatches surrounding the swatch of interest. Photocopy or download from the website and print out.

*For additional information on the book and any updates, please visit: www.**pelemeleworks**.com*

If you have a question, spot a mistake, or anything else, you are welcome to **get in touch** through the website. Support Pêle-Mêle Works titles and **write a review** on Amazon or elsewhere. Thank you!

USING THE SWATCH GRIDS

Values for colours (any CMYK except for K=100) are grouped together.

- Values for **C and M are constant** for the grid and are indicated at the bottom of the grid.
- Values for **Y vary from left to right** from 0 to 100 in steps of 10.
- Values for **K vary from top to bottom** from 0 to 90 in steps of 10.

For the swatch on the grid, its CMYK value is:

- C and M are the grid values: C=40 and M=10.
- Y is the column value: Y=60.
- K is the row value: K=20.

The full CMYK value is: 40C 10M 60Y 20K.

This grid features values 40-10-0-0 to 40-10-100-90.

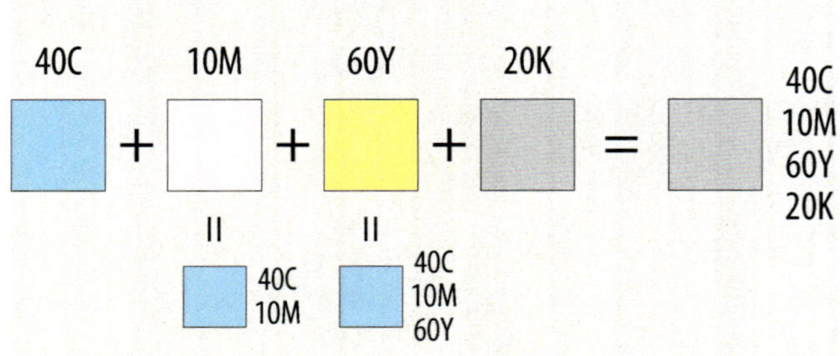

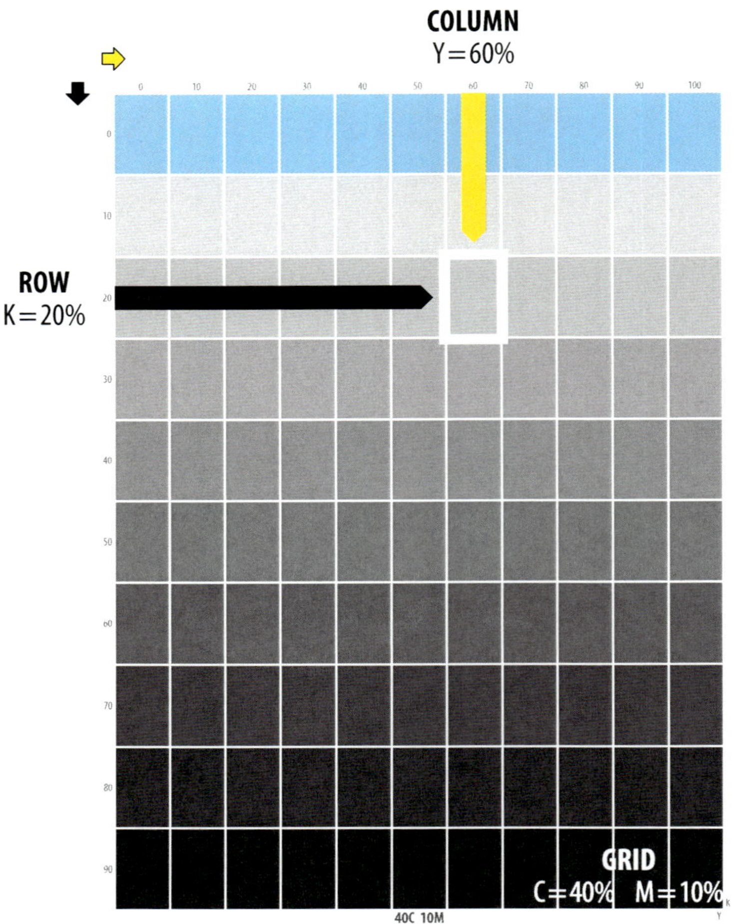

Values for blacks (K=100, any CMY) are grouped in a section of their own.

- Values for **C and K are constant** for the grid and are indicated at the bottom of the grid.
- Values for **M vary from left to right** from 0 to 100 in steps of 10.
- Values for **Y vary from top to bottom** from 0 to 100 in steps of 10.

For the swatch on the grid, its CMYK value is:

- C is the grid value: C=0.
- M is the column value: M=30.
- Y is the row value: Y=50.
- K is constant: K=100.

The full CMYK value is: 0C 30M 50Y 100K.

This grid features values 0-0-0-100 to 0-100-100-100.

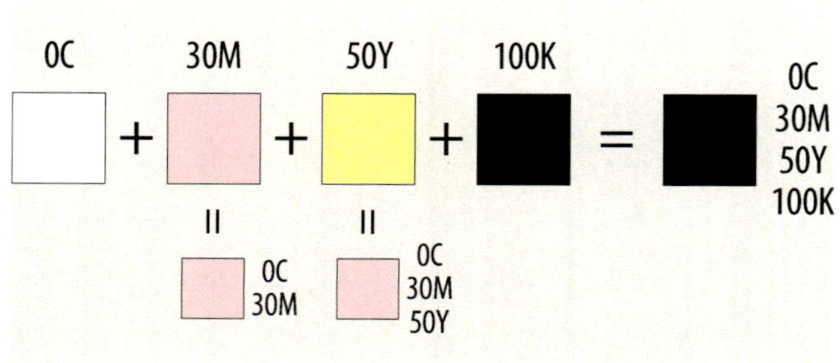

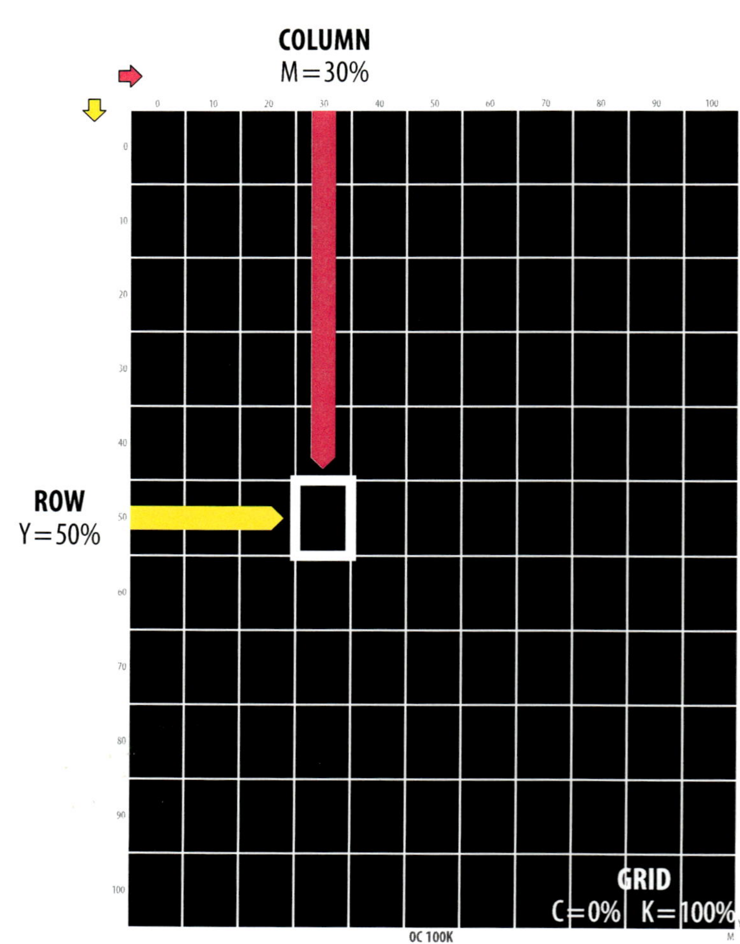

TINTS

C
M
Y
K
CMY tonality & grey balance
5
10
15
20
25
30
35
40
45
50
55
60
65
70
75
80
85
90
95
100
25 19 19 0
50 40 40 0
75 66 66 0

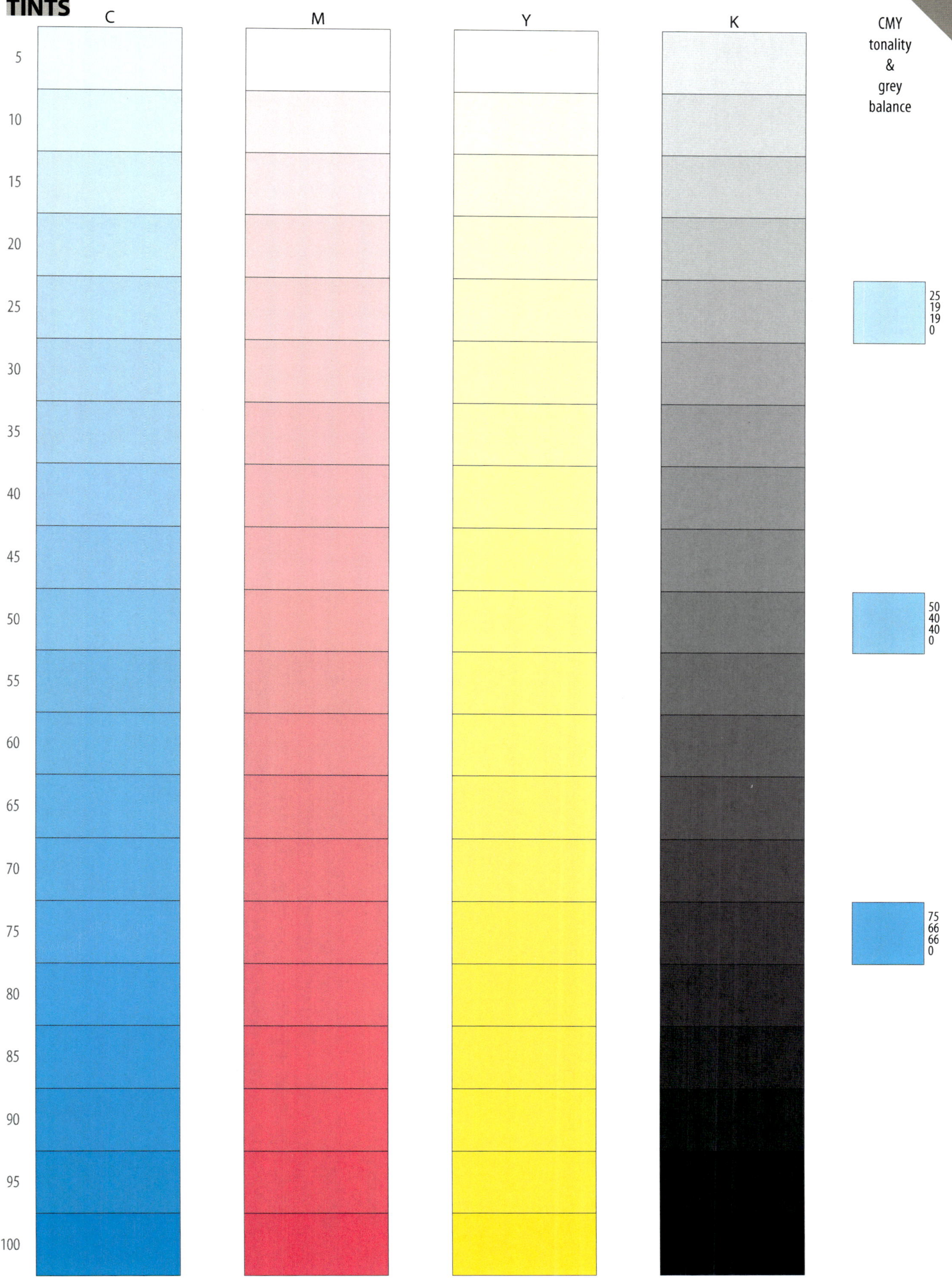

FINE STEP TINTS

1–100 in steps of 1 | row + column = ink value

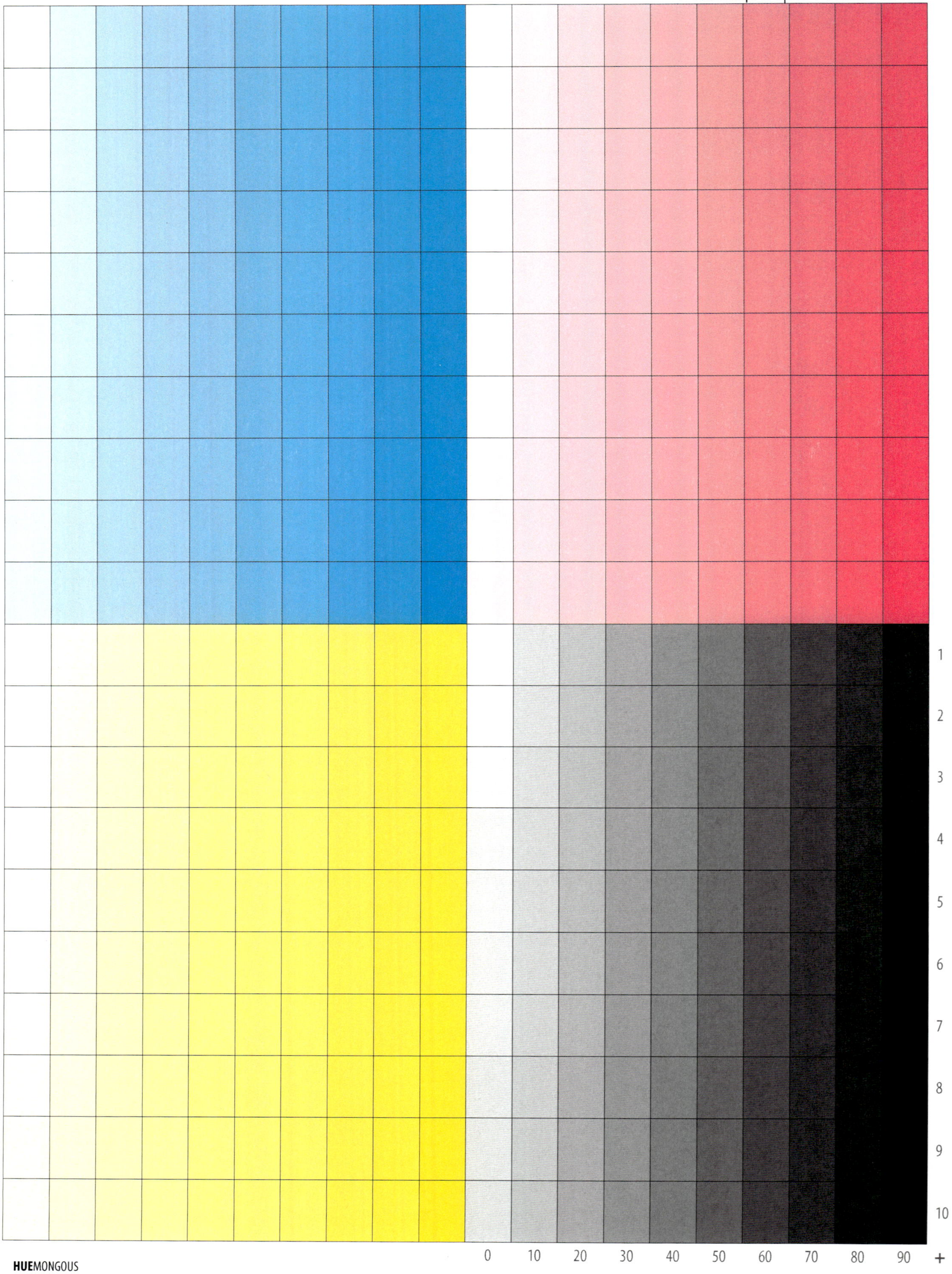

										1
										2
										3
										4
										5
										6
										7
										8
										9
										10
0	10	20	30	40	50	60	70	80	90	+

GRADIENTS

COLOUR WHEEL

The colour wheel is built by gradually increasing and decreasing the value of each ink (CMY) and blending each ink with one other ink at a time. There is no black ink (K) in the colour mix. The wheel starts with solid Cyan 100 0 0 0, right before 12 o'clock, and ends on 100 0 10 0, cycling in steps of 10, anticlockwise.

By breaking up the wheel and unrolling it flat, a linear arrangement of those colours is obtained. This is the basis for the diagram below. The "flattened wheel" is placed in the middle of the diagram, with the label 0, and serves as the reference for the other colours.

In the upper half of the diagram, the reference colours are gradually made lighter by reducing the value of each ink (CMY) in equal proportions. This produces **tints** of each colour in steps of 10 percentage points (from 10% to 90% reduction of the reference colours).

In the lower half of the diagram, black ink (K) is gradually added to the reference colours. This produces **shades** of each colour in steps of 10 percentage points (from 10% to 90% of added black ink).

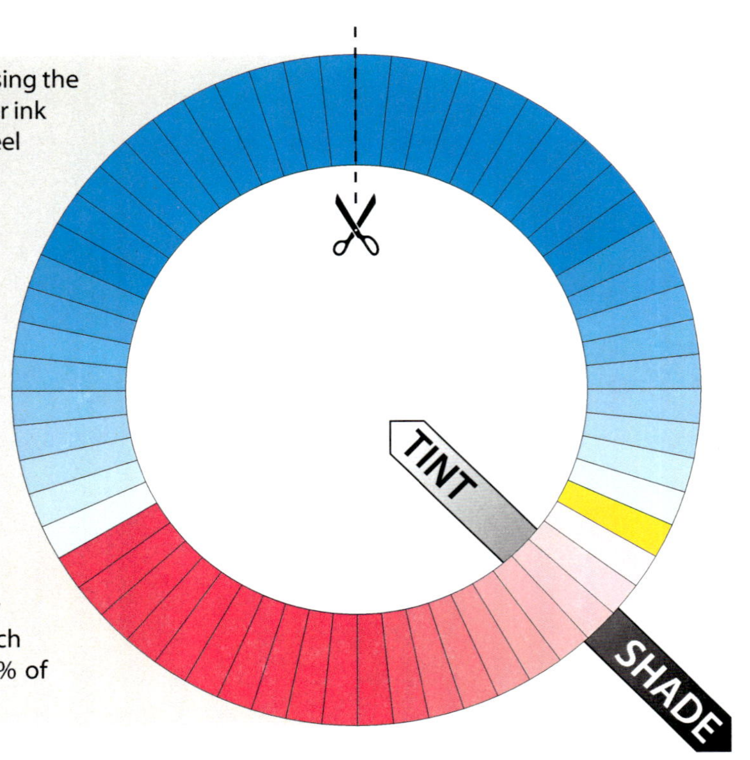

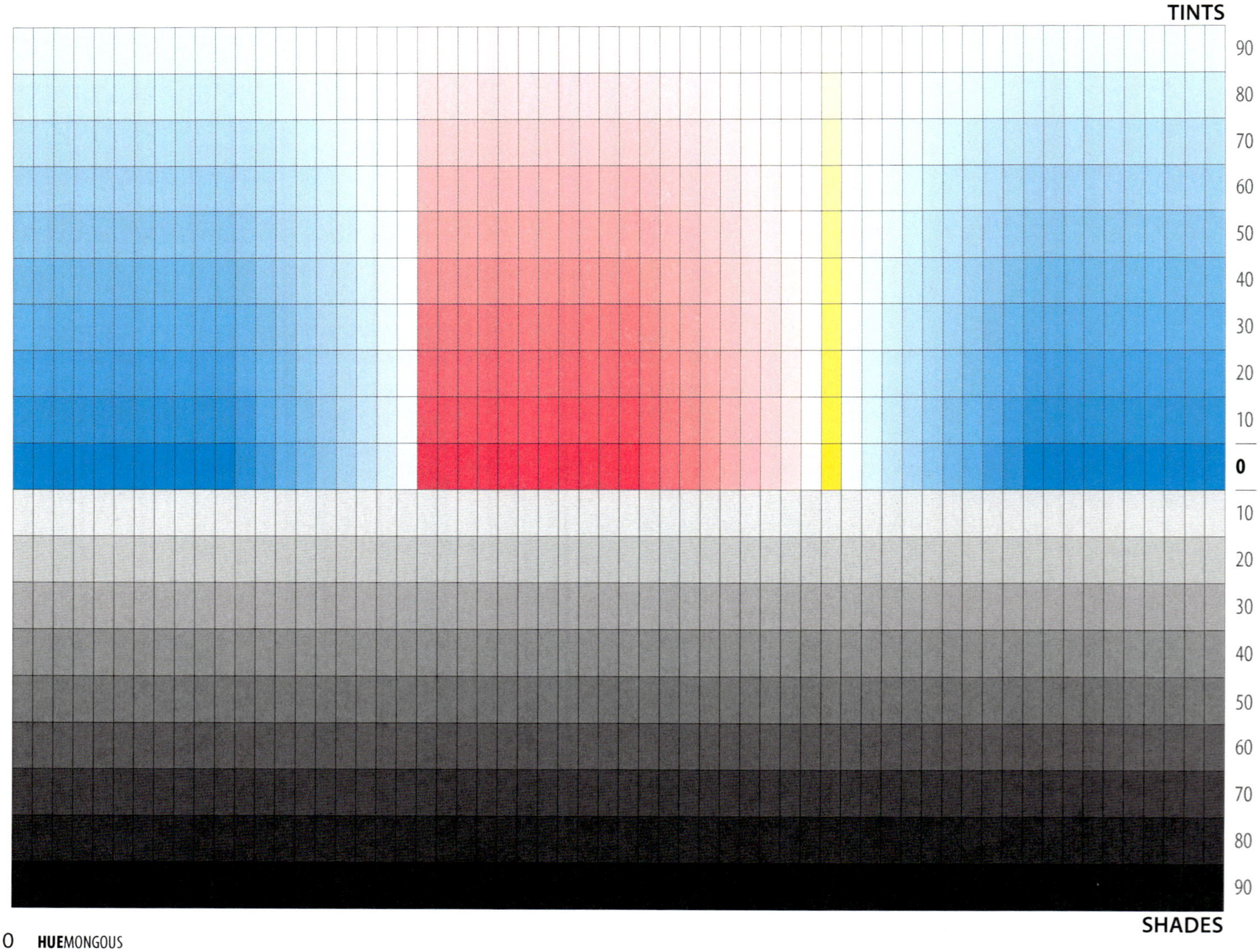

TINTS
90
80
70
60
50
40
30
20
10
0
10
20
30
40
50
60
70
80
90
SHADES

SHADES OF BLACK

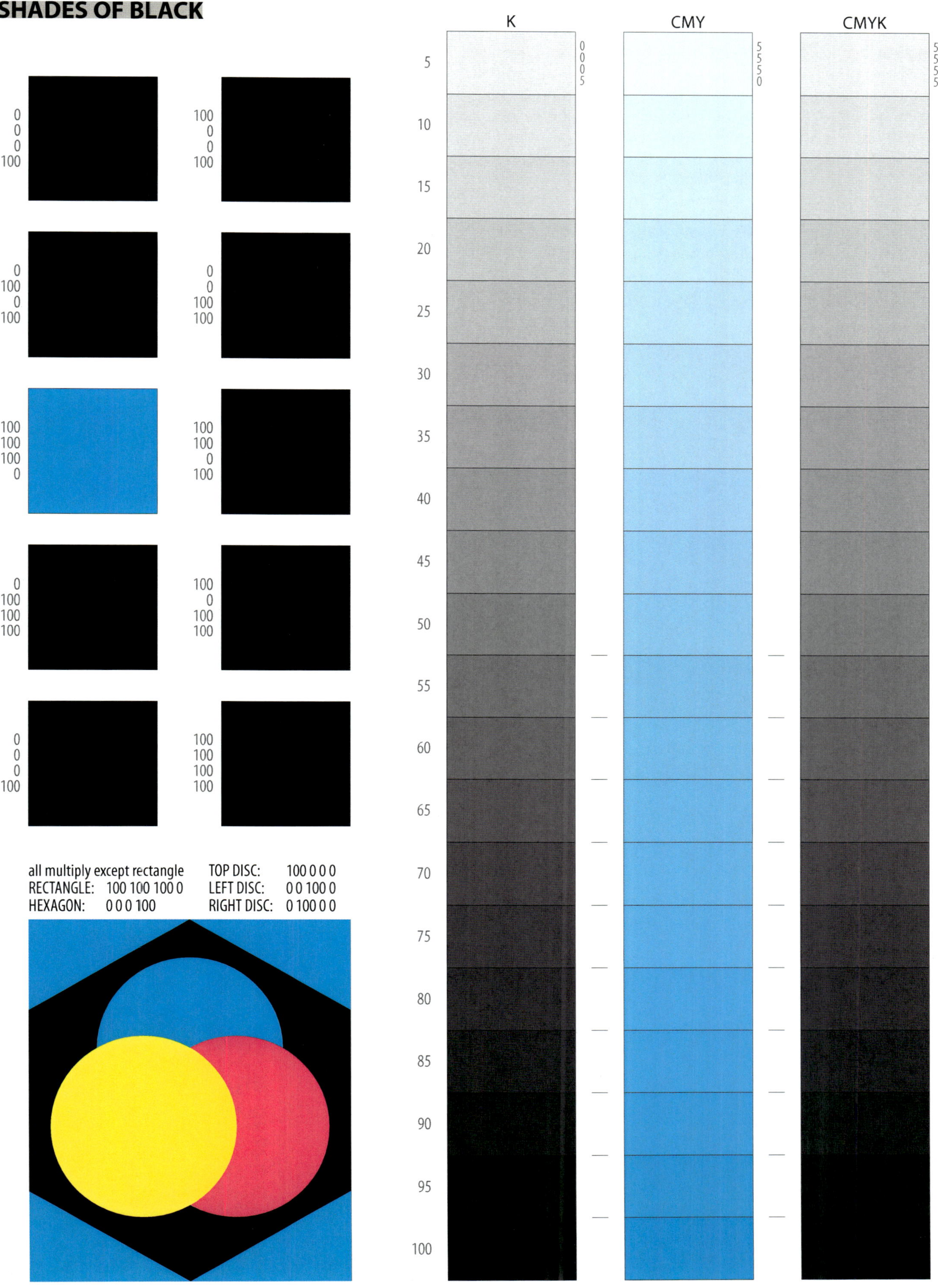

BLACK SUBSTITUTION

Black ink can be used to substitute for neutral amounts of CMY inks (grey). This operation achieves visually satisfactory results with the modified colour being close enough to the original colour. Some of the benefits of resorting to such substitution are to reduce ink consumption and to lessen the overall impact of colour variations during manufacturing (turns a threefold variation in C, M, and Y inks into a onefold variation in K ink).

The example shows a CMY swatch made of 50C 50M 50Y 0K and corresponding swatches where some proportion of CMY is replaced by increasing amounts of black. For each swatch, Total Ink Coverage (TIC) is indicated after the CMYK values. Proportions must be adjusted to achieve the desired result and need not necessarily follow a 1C 1M 1Y to 1K ratio or a linear relationship. Conversely, the reverse operation (substitute CMY for K) also makes sense in some situations. For instance, it can make a colour less dull or mitigate misregistration (if the element of interest is surrounded by CMY). Black substitution can be applied to any CMYK colour containing CMY or K, as demonstrated by the second set of swatches.

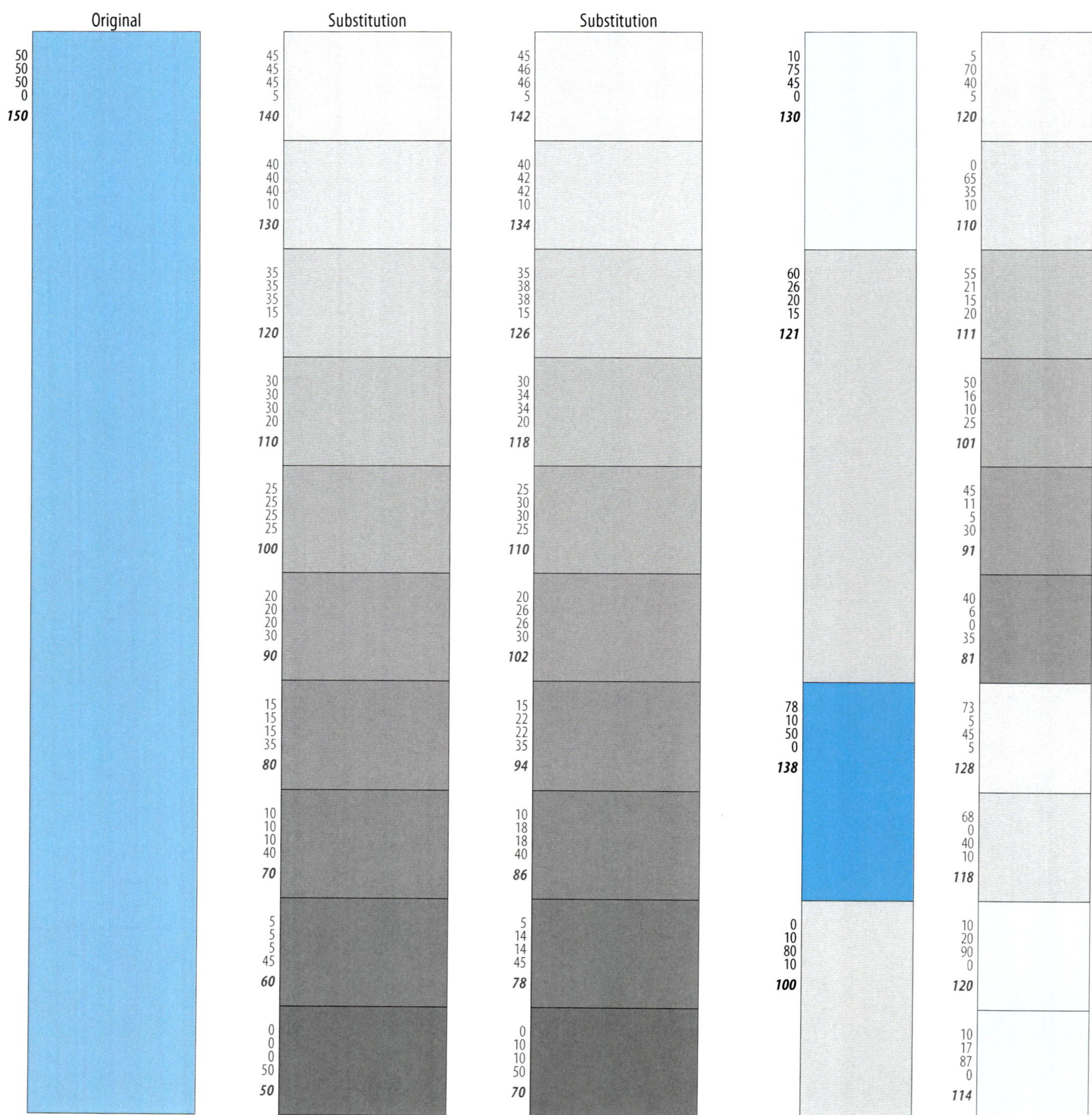

OVERPRINT

T: top, m: middle, B: bottom

CMY overprinting

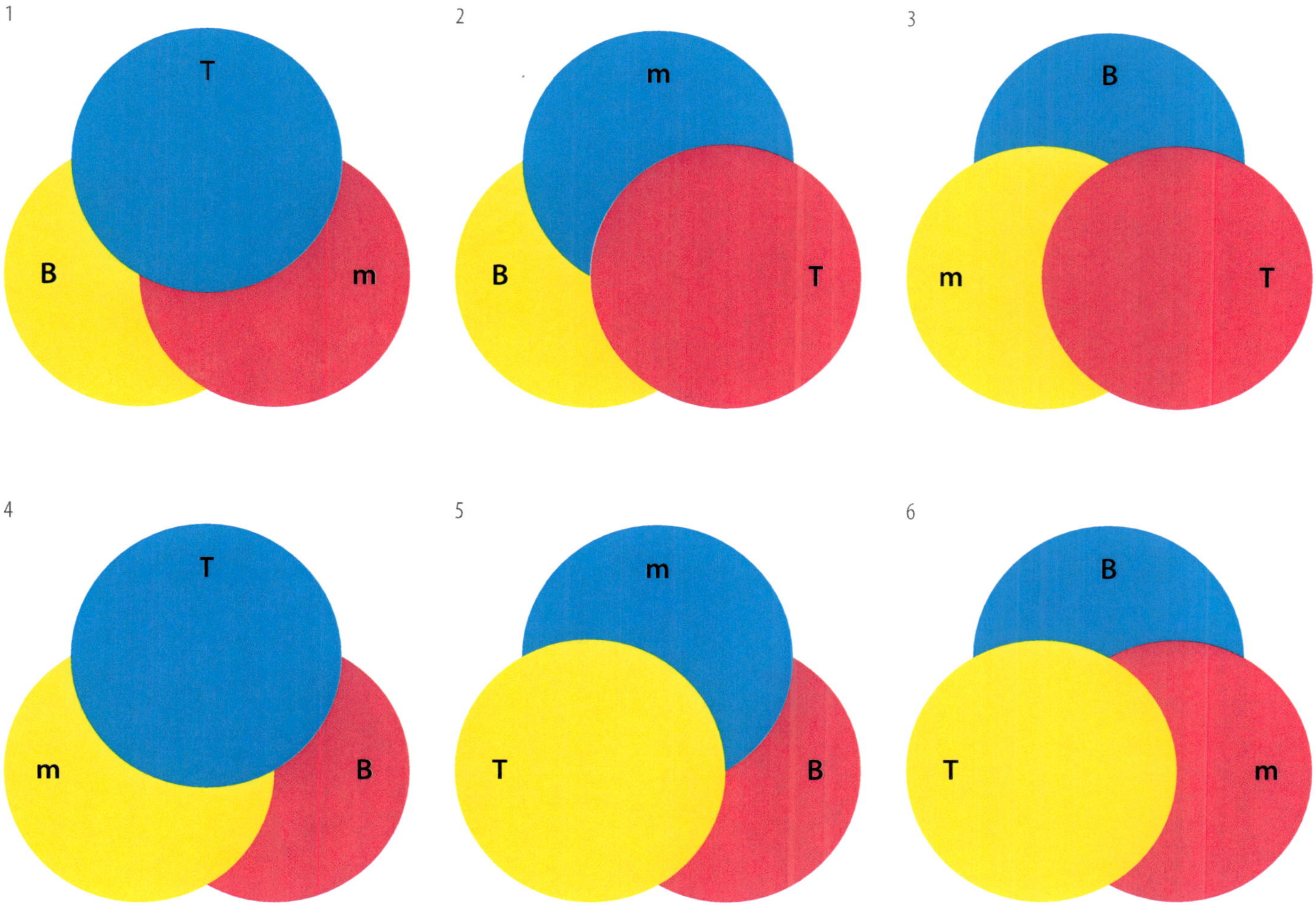

1
T
B
m

2
m
B
T

3
B
m
T

4
T
m
B

5
m
T
B

6
B
T
m

BLACK OVERPRINT

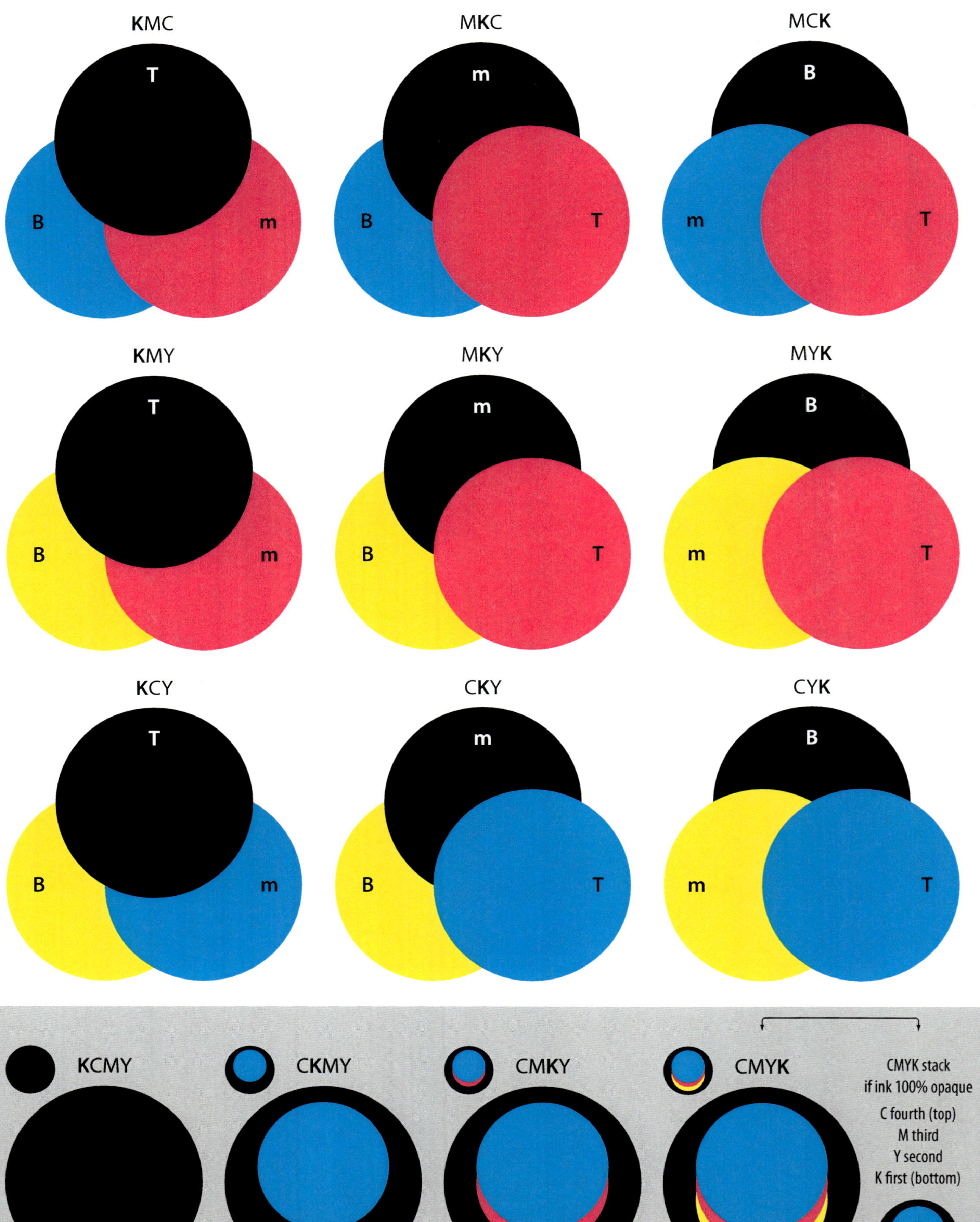

MULTIPLY VS. OVERPRINT

Multiplying and overprinting are two concepts that can be confusing or misunderstood, and therefore misused. Both concepts operate on each ink separately and independently. Both concepts fully operate in the chosen colour space (CMYK in this case), from start to finish. Let's formalise each. To do this, we place an element B of colour B_C B_M B_Y B_K on the bottom and an element T of colour T_C T_M T_Y T_K on top. The top element T is set to multiply, then set to overprint. The result R of the area where B and T overlap is of colour R_C R_M R_Y R_K. The formulas show how to get from B and T to R for the Cyan ink (C). The same formulas apply to the other inks.

MULTIPLY

$$R_C = T_C \times (1 - B_C) + B_C$$

OVERPRINT

$$\text{if } T_C > 0,\ R_C = T_C \text{ else } R_C = B_C$$

Each ink value is first reduced from 0–100 to 0–1 by dividing it by 100. The formula is then applied to the reduced value in the range 0–1. The result is multiplied by 100 to bring it back to an ink value in the range 0–100.

- For multiply, R_C can also be written as $R_C = B_C \times (1 - T_C) + T_C$. The top and bottom colours are interchangeable. This is not the case for overprint.
- Because a positive value is added to B_C (or T_C), multiply always produces a "darker" colour (greater ink value) than both bottom and top colours. If $T_C = 0$, $R_C = B_C$. If $T_C = 100$ ($T_C = 1$ in the formula), $R_C = 100$. So white 0C 0M 0Y 0K multiplying any colour X results in X. Black 0C 0M 0Y 100K multiplying any colour X results in a variant of black (X_C X_M X_Y 100K).
- Overprint is like an on/off switch: the result is either the top or the bottom colour, not any other ink value. It is less processing-intensive than multiply.
- Multiply lets some of the bottom ink "show through" the top (same) ink, overprint does not (it's all or nothing). Multiply is therefore associated with the concept of *transparency*, overprint is not.
- Overprint can be counter-intuitive in some cases. For example, if the top colour T_C is "lighter" than the bottom colour B_C ($0 < T_C < B_C$), overprinting T_C on B_C results in T_C. Effectively, T_C is "knocking out" B_C more so than "printing over" B_C! The overprinting ink can be thought of as opaque.

The examples illustrate how the two operations can yield similar or very different results. Square B is on the bottom and disc T is on top. B is always clear of any fill attributes, it is T's fill that is alternately set to multiply and to overprint. Take note of the stroke of the square showing or not through the centre of the disc. The stroke is made of 0C 0M 0Y 100K and is a telltale sign of transparency in multiply and of the toggle switch nature of overprint ($T_K = 0$ or $T_K \neq 0$).

Remember that we are working with a four-ink process to generate the desired colour, not directly with the desired colour as an ink by itself (a *spot colour*, in printing terms).

Probe this topic further: 1- would it make sense to set the top element to both multiply and overprint?, 2- add a third element on top of the other two and set it to multiply or overprint, 3- multiply and overprint CMYK with spot colours.

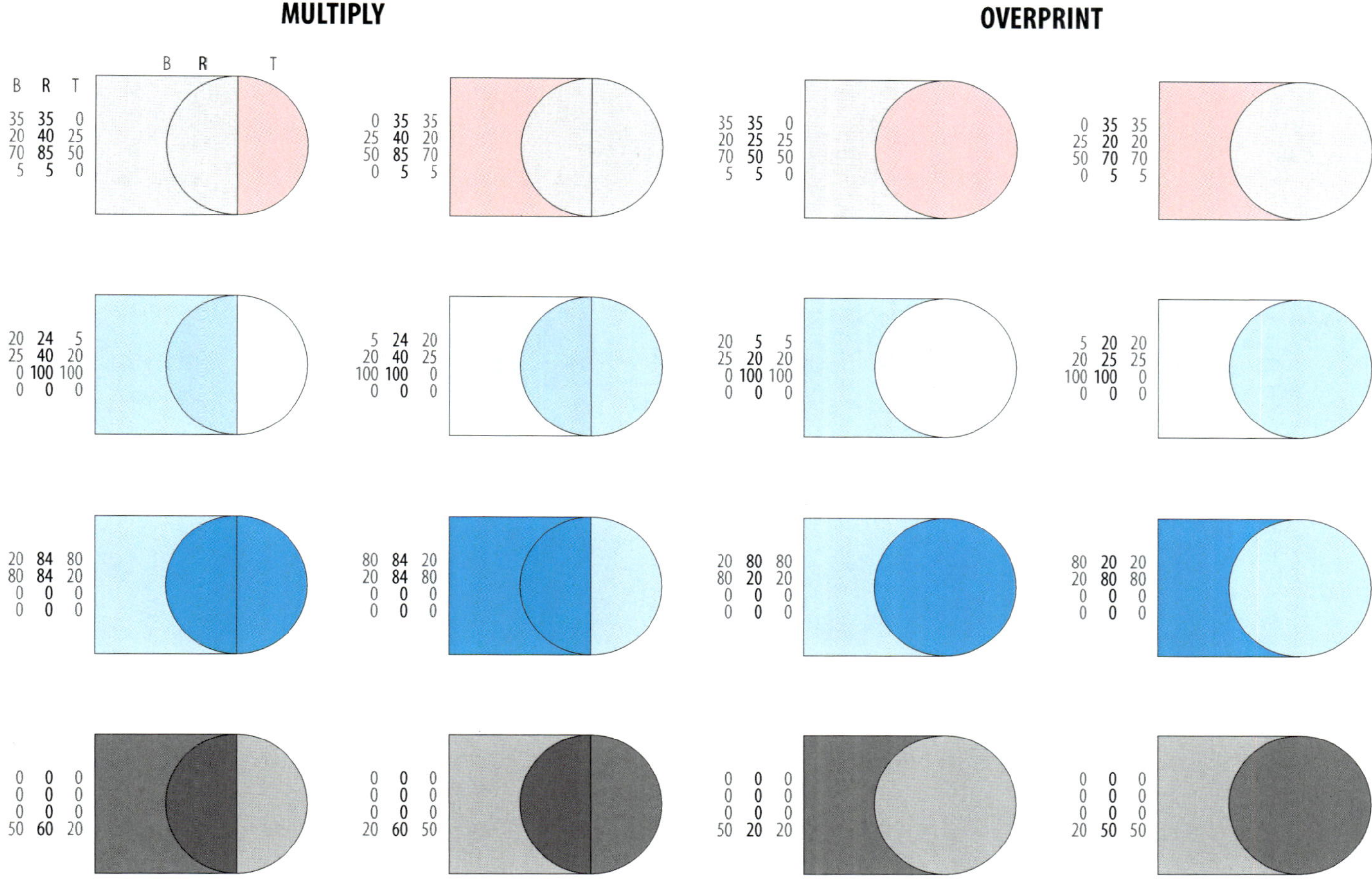

DOTS

Discs, squares, triangles (pt)

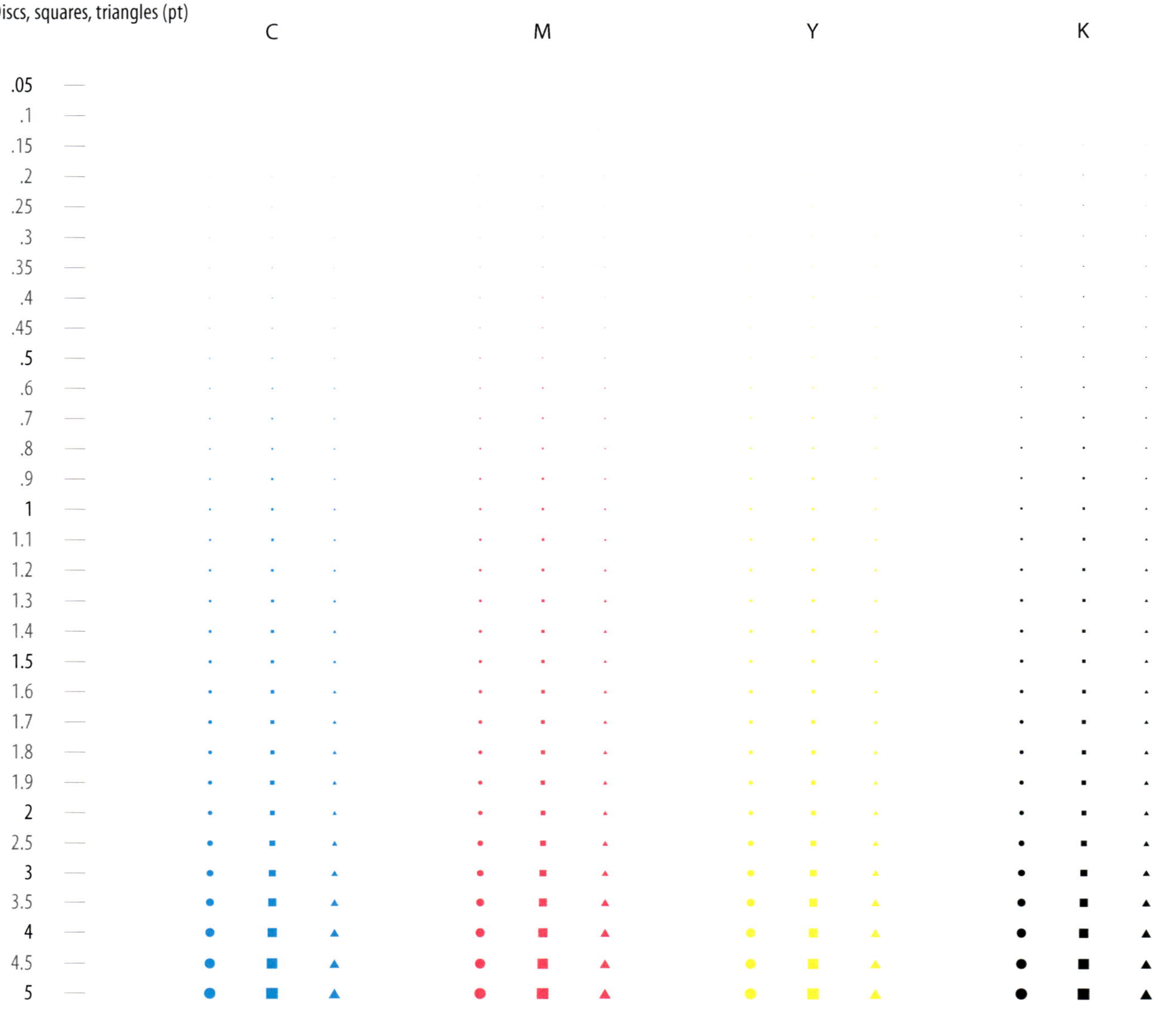

C M Y K

.05
.1
.15
.2
.25
.3
.35
.4
.45
.5
.6
.7
.8
.9
1
1.1
1.2
1.3
1.4
1.5
1.6
1.7
1.8
1.9
2
2.5
3
3.5
4
4.5
5

Polygons 3–20 points (5 pt radius)

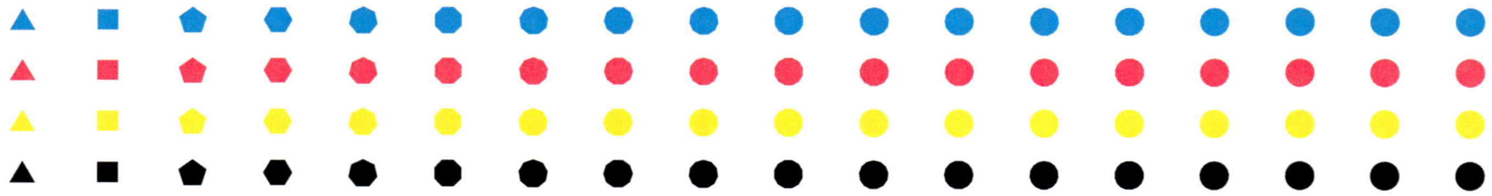

Star polygons 3–20 points (5 pt / 2.5 pt radii)

RULES

Rule lines (pt)

C

.01
.02
.05
.1
.15
.2
.25
.3
.35
.4

.41
.45
.5
.55
.6
.65
.7
.75
.8
1

1.05
1.5
2
2.1
3
3.5
5

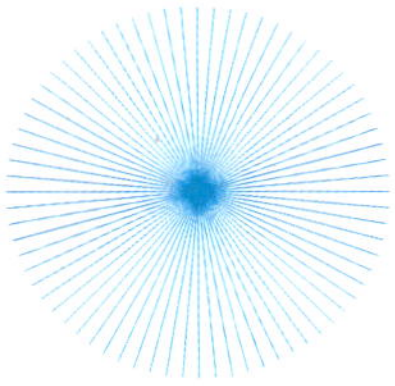

0.25 pt in 5 deg. steps

M

.01
.02
.05
.1
.15
.2
.25
.3
.35
.4

.41
.45
.5
.55
.6
.65
.7
.75
.8
1

1.05
1.5
2
2.1
3
3.5
5

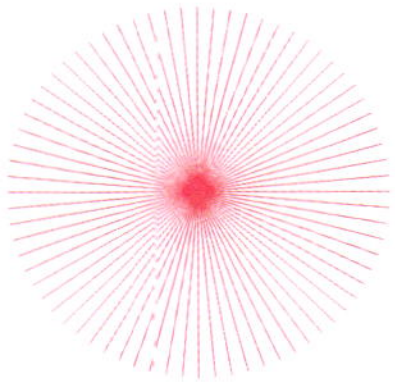

Y

.01 .02 .05 .1 .15 .2 .25 .3 .35 .4

.41 .45 .5 .55 .6 .65 .7 .75 .8 1

1.05 1.5 2 2.1 3 3.5 5

K

.01 .02 .05 .1 .15 .2 .25 .3 .35 .4

.41 .45 .5 .55 .6 .65 .7 .75 .8 1

1.05 1.5 2 2.1 3 3.5 5

TYPE

Times New Roman font (pt)

pt			pt
14	abcdefghijklmnopqrstuvwxyzABCDEFGHIJKLMNOPQRSTUVWXYZ0123456789		
13	abcdefghijklmnopqrstuvwxyzABCDEFGHIJKLMNOPQRSTUVWXYZ0123456789		
12	abcdefghijklmnopqrstuvwxyzABCDEFGHIJKLMNOPQRSTUVWXYZ0123456789		
11	abcdefghijklmnopqrstuvwxyzABCDEFGHIJKLMNOPQRSTUVWXYZ0123456789	abcdefghijklmnopqrstuvwxyzABCDEFGHIJKLMNOPQRSTUVWXYZ0123456789	1
10	abcdefghijklmnopqrstuvwxyzABCDEFGHIJKLMNOPQRSTUVWXYZ0123456789	abcdefghijklmnopqrstuvwxyzABCDEFGHIJKLMNOPQRSTUVWXYZ0123456789	2
9	abcdefghijklmnopqrstuvwxyzABCDEFGHIJKLMNOPQRSTUVWXYZ0123456789	abcdefghijklmnopqrstuvwxyzABCDEFGHIJKLMNOPQRSTUVWXYZ0123456789	3
8	abcdefghijklmnopqrstuvwxyzABCDEFGHIJKLMNOPQRSTUVWXYZ0123456789	abcdefghijklmnopqrstuvwxyzABCDEFGHIJKLMNOPQRSTUVWXYZ0123456789	4
7	abcdefghijklmnopqrstuvwxyzABCDEFGHIJKLMNOPQRSTUVWXYZ0123456789	abcdefghijklmnopqrstuvwxyzABCDEFGHIJKLMNOPQRSTUVWXYZ0123456789	5
6	abcdefghijklmnopqrstuvwxyzABCDEFGHIJKLMNOPQRSTUVWXYZ0123456789	abcdefghijklmnopqrstuvwxyzABCDEFGHIJKLMNOPQRSTUVWXYZ0123456789	6
5	abcdefghijklmnopqrstuvwxyzABCDEFGHIJKLMNOPQRSTUVWXYZ0123456789	abcdefghijklmnopqrstuvwxyzABCDEFGHIJKLMNOPQRSTUVWXYZ0123456789	7
4	abcdefghijklmnopqrstuvwxyzABCDEFGHIJKLMNOPQRSTUVWXYZ0123456789	abcdefghijklmnopqrstuvwxyzABCDEFGHIJKLMNOPQRSTUVWXYZ0123456789	8
3	abcdefghijklmnopqrstuvwxyzABCDEFGHIJKLMNOPQRSTUVWXYZ0123456789	abcdefghijklmnopqrstuvwxyzABCDEFGHIJKLMNOPQRSTUVWXYZ0123456789	9
2	abcdefghijklmnopqrstuvwxyzABCDEFGHIJKLMNOPQRSTUVWXYZ0123456789	abcdefghijklmnopqrstuvwxyzABCDEFGHIJKLMNOPQRSTUVWXYZ0123456789	10
1	abcdefghijklmnopqrstuvwxyzABCDEFGHIJKLMNOPQRSTUVWXYZ0123456789	abcdefghijklmnopqrstuvwxyzABCDEFGHIJKLMNOPQRSTUVWXYZ0123456789	11
		abcdefghijklmnopqrstuvwxyzABCDEFGHIJKLMNOPQRSTUVWXYZ0123456789	12
		abcdefghijklmnopqrstuvwxyzABCDEFGHIJKLMNOPQRSTUVWXYZ0123456789	13
		abcdefghijklmnopqrstuvwxyzABCDEFGHIJKLMNOPQRSTUVWXYZ0123456789	14

pt			pt
14	abcdefghijklmnopqrstuvwxyzABCDEFGHIJKLMNOPQRSTUVWXYZ0123456789		
13	abcdefghijklmnopqrstuvwxyzABCDEFGHIJKLMNOPQRSTUVWXYZ0123456789		
12	abcdefghijklmnopqrstuvwxyzABCDEFGHIJKLMNOPQRSTUVWXYZ0123456789		
11	abcdefghijklmnopqrstuvwxyzABCDEFGHIJKLMNOPQRSTUVWXYZ0123456789	abcdefghijklmnopqrstuvwxyzABCDEFGHIJKLMNOPQRSTUVWXYZ0123456789	1
10	abcdefghijklmnopqrstuvwxyzABCDEFGHIJKLMNOPQRSTUVWXYZ0123456789	abcdefghijklmnopqrstuvwxyzABCDEFGHIJKLMNOPQRSTUVWXYZ0123456789	2
9	abcdefghijklmnopqrstuvwxyzABCDEFGHIJKLMNOPQRSTUVWXYZ0123456789	abcdefghijklmnopqrstuvwxyzABCDEFGHIJKLMNOPQRSTUVWXYZ0123456789	3
8	abcdefghijklmnopqrstuvwxyzABCDEFGHIJKLMNOPQRSTUVWXYZ0123456789	abcdefghijklmnopqrstuvwxyzABCDEFGHIJKLMNOPQRSTUVWXYZ0123456789	4
7	abcdefghijklmnopqrstuvwxyzABCDEFGHIJKLMNOPQRSTUVWXYZ0123456789	abcdefghijklmnopqrstuvwxyzABCDEFGHIJKLMNOPQRSTUVWXYZ0123456789	5
6	abcdefghijklmnopqrstuvwxyzABCDEFGHIJKLMNOPQRSTUVWXYZ0123456789	abcdefghijklmnopqrstuvwxyzABCDEFGHIJKLMNOPQRSTUVWXYZ0123456789	6
5	abcdefghijklmnopqrstuvwxyzABCDEFGHIJKLMNOPQRSTUVWXYZ0123456789	abcdefghijklmnopqrstuvwxyzABCDEFGHIJKLMNOPQRSTUVWXYZ0123456789	7
4	abcdefghijklmnopqrstuvwxyzABCDEFGHIJKLMNOPQRSTUVWXYZ0123456789	abcdefghijklmnopqrstuvwxyzABCDEFGHIJKLMNOPQRSTUVWXYZ0123456789	8
3	abcdefghijklmnopqrstuvwxyzABCDEFGHIJKLMNOPQRSTUVWXYZ0123456789	abcdefghijklmnopqrstuvwxyzABCDEFGHIJKLMNOPQRSTUVWXYZ0123456789	9
2	abcdefghijklmnopqrstuvwxyzABCDEFGHIJKLMNOPQRSTUVWXYZ0123456789	abcdefghijklmnopqrstuvwxyzABCDEFGHIJKLMNOPQRSTUVWXYZ0123456789	10
1	abcdefghijklmnopqrstuvwxyzABCDEFGHIJKLMNOPQRSTUVWXYZ0123456789	abcdefghijklmnopqrstuvwxyzABCDEFGHIJKLMNOPQRSTUVWXYZ0123456789	11
		abcdefghijklmnopqrstuvwxyzABCDEFGHIJKLMNOPQRSTUVWXYZ0123456789	12
		abcdefghijklmnopqrstuvwxyzABCDEFGHIJKLMNOPQRSTUVWXYZ0123456789	13
		abcdefghijklmnopqrstuvwxyzABCDEFGHIJKLMNOPQRSTUVWXYZ0123456789	14

12 pt Times New Roman

Regular	abcdefghijklmnopqrstuvwxyzABCDEFGHIJKLMNOPQRSTUVWXYZ0123456789
Regular outlined	abcdefghijklmnopqrstuvwxyzABCDEFGHIJKLMNOPQRSTUVWXYZ0123456789
Italic	*abcdefghijklmnopqrstuvwxyzABCDEFGHIJKLMNOPQRSTUVWXYZ0123456789*
Bold	**abcdefghijklmnopqrstuvwxyzABCDEFGHIJKLMNOPQRSTUVWXYZ0123456789**
Bold Italic	***abcdefghijklmnopqrstuvwxyzABCDEFGHIJKLMNOPQRSTUVWXYZ0123456789***

RULE AND TYPE TINTS

12 pt font | .25–2 pt rules in .25 pt steps

C	M	Y	K	Tint
abcdefghijklmno			abcdefghijklmno	
pqrstuvwxyz012			pqrstuvwxyz012	
3456789ABCDE			3456789ABCDE	10
FGHIJKLMNOP			FGHIJKLMNOP	
QRSTUVWXYZ			QRSTUVWXYZ	
abcdefghijklmno	abcdefghijklmno	abcdefghijklmno	abcdefghijklmno	
pqrstuvwxyz012	pqrstuvwxyz012	pqrstuvwxyz012	pqrstuvwxyz012	
3456789ABCDE	3456789ABCDE	3456789ABCDE	3456789ABCDE	20
FGHIJKLMNOP	FGHIJKLMNOP	FGHIJKLMNOP	FGHIJKLMNOP	
QRSTUVWXYZ	QRSTUVWXYZ	QRSTUVWXYZ	QRSTUVWXYZ	
abcdefghijklmno	abcdefghijklmno	abcdefghijklmno	abcdefghijklmno	
pqrstuvwxyz012	pqrstuvwxyz012	pqrstuvwxyz012	pqrstuvwxyz012	
3456789ABCDE	3456789ABCDE	3456789ABCDE	3456789ABCDE	30
FGHIJKLMNOP	FGHIJKLMNOP	FGHIJKLMNOP	FGHIJKLMNOP	
QRSTUVWXYZ	QRSTUVWXYZ	QRSTUVWXYZ	QRSTUVWXYZ	
abcdefghijklmno	abcdefghijklmno	abcdefghijklmno	abcdefghijklmno	
pqrstuvwxyz012	pqrstuvwxyz012	pqrstuvwxyz012	pqrstuvwxyz012	
3456789ABCDE	3456789ABCDE	3456789ABCDE	3456789ABCDE	40
FGHIJKLMNOP	FGHIJKLMNOP	FGHIJKLMNOP	FGHIJKLMNOP	
QRSTUVWXYZ	QRSTUVWXYZ	QRSTUVWXYZ	QRSTUVWXYZ	
abcdefghijklmno	abcdefghijklmno	abcdefghijklmno	abcdefghijklmno	
pqrstuvwxyz012	pqrstuvwxyz012	pqrstuvwxyz012	pqrstuvwxyz012	
3456789ABCDE	3456789ABCDE	3456789ABCDE	3456789ABCDE	50
FGHIJKLMNOP	FGHIJKLMNOP	FGHIJKLMNOP	FGHIJKLMNOP	
QRSTUVWXYZ	QRSTUVWXYZ	QRSTUVWXYZ	QRSTUVWXYZ	
abcdefghijklmno	abcdefghijklmno	abcdefghijklmno	abcdefghijklmno	
pqrstuvwxyz012	pqrstuvwxyz012	pqrstuvwxyz012	pqrstuvwxyz012	
3456789ABCDE	3456789ABCDE	3456789ABCDE	3456789ABCDE	60
FGHIJKLMNOP	FGHIJKLMNOP	FGHIJKLMNOP	FGHIJKLMNOP	
QRSTUVWXYZ	QRSTUVWXYZ	QRSTUVWXYZ	QRSTUVWXYZ	
abcdefghijklmno	abcdefghijklmno	abcdefghijklmno	abcdefghijklmno	
pqrstuvwxyz012	pqrstuvwxyz012	pqrstuvwxyz012	pqrstuvwxyz012	
3456789ABCDE	3456789ABCDE	3456789ABCDE	3456789ABCDE	70
FGHIJKLMNOP	FGHIJKLMNOP	FGHIJKLMNOP	FGHIJKLMNOP	
QRSTUVWXYZ	QRSTUVWXYZ	QRSTUVWXYZ	QRSTUVWXYZ	
abcdefghijklmno	abcdefghijklmno	abcdefghijklmno	abcdefghijklmno	
pqrstuvwxyz012	pqrstuvwxyz012	pqrstuvwxyz012	pqrstuvwxyz012	
3456789ABCDE	3456789ABCDE	3456789ABCDE	3456789ABCDE	80
FGHIJKLMNOP	FGHIJKLMNOP	FGHIJKLMNOP	FGHIJKLMNOP	
QRSTUVWXYZ	QRSTUVWXYZ	QRSTUVWXYZ	QRSTUVWXYZ	
abcdefghijklmno	abcdefghijklmno	abcdefghijklmno	abcdefghijklmno	
pqrstuvwxyz012	pqrstuvwxyz012	pqrstuvwxyz012	pqrstuvwxyz012	
3456789ABCDE	3456789ABCDE	3456789ABCDE	3456789ABCDE	90
FGHIJKLMNOP	FGHIJKLMNOP	FGHIJKLMNOP	FGHIJKLMNOP	
QRSTUVWXYZ	QRSTUVWXYZ	QRSTUVWXYZ	QRSTUVWXYZ	
abcdefghijklmno	abcdefghijklmno	abcdefghijklmno	abcdefghijklmno	
pqrstuvwxyz012	pqrstuvwxyz012	pqrstuvwxyz012	pqrstuvwxyz012	
3456789ABCDE	3456789ABCDE	3456789ABCDE	3456789ABCDE	100
FGHIJKLMNOP	FGHIJKLMNOP	FGHIJKLMNOP	FGHIJKLMNOP	
QRSTUVWXYZ	QRSTUVWXYZ	QRSTUVWXYZ	QRSTUVWXYZ	

INK SPREAD

rules in pt

Ink spread (top) | Registration (bottom)

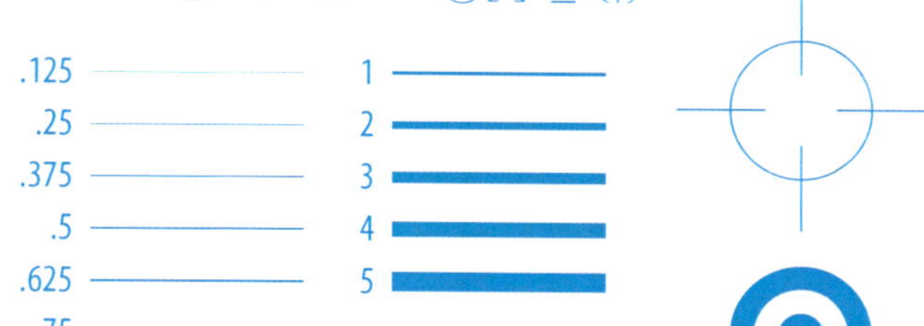

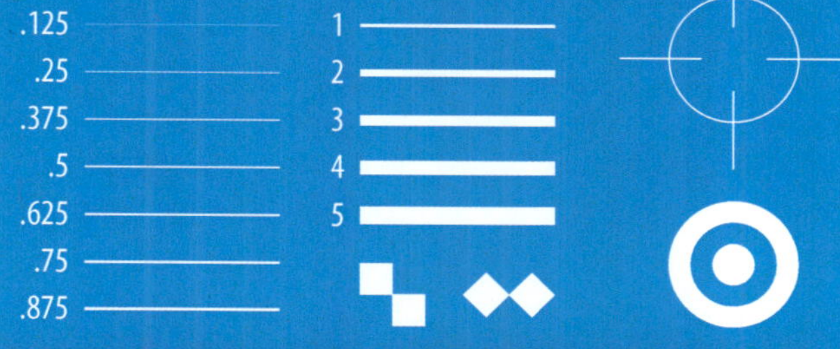

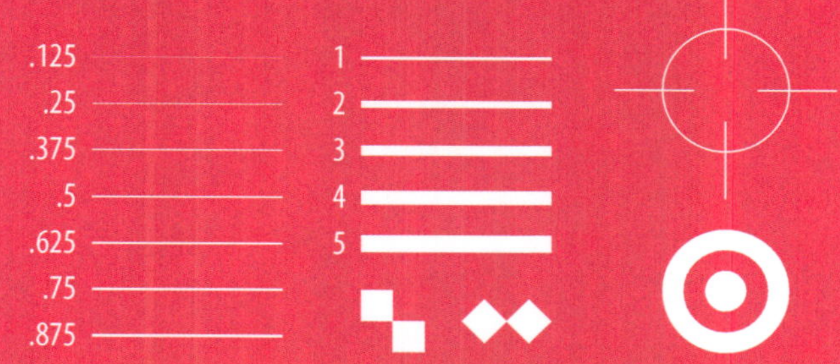

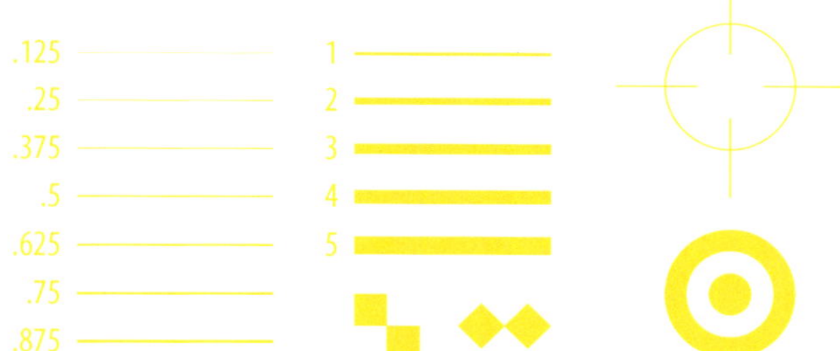

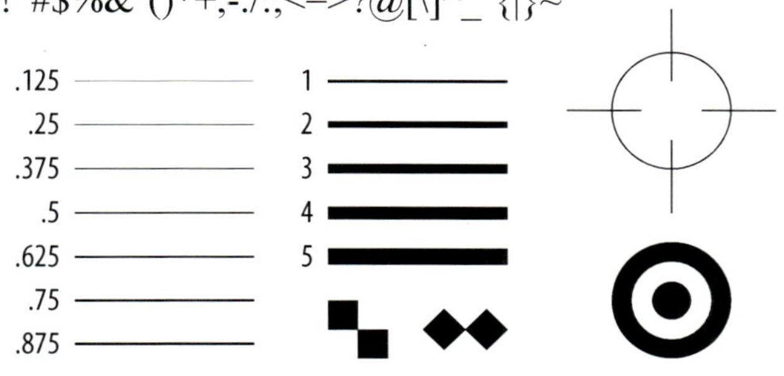

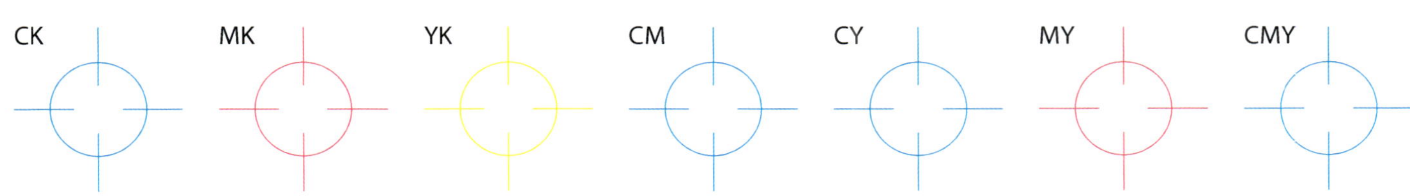

COLOUR MATCHING

The step size for ink value increments is 10%. This means that any colour X, defined by its CMYK values (X_C X_M X_Y X_K), will fall between two ink values in the swatch grids, 10 points apart. What can this difference look like in practice? The following example illustrates the delta between a colour X, unavailable in the grids, and its closest colour swatches in the grids. The CMYK values for X are 25C 17M 72Y 6K. Each of these values is bound by two ink values in the swatch grids; that is a total of $2^4 = 16$ swatches nearing colour X. In the example, X_C, the Cyan ink value for X, is 25 and is bound by values 20 and 30 in the grids. For all four inks, bounding values are:

$$20 \leq X_C = 25 \leq 30,$$
$$10 \leq X_M = 17 \leq 20,$$
$$70 \leq X_Y = 72 \leq 80,$$
$$0 \leq X_K = 6 \leq 10.$$

In the diagram below, the 16 bounding swatches are placed within the larger swatch, representing the colour of interest X. These 16 colours are the closest matches to colour X. Visually, colour deltas will be more or less pronounced depending on the colours involved.

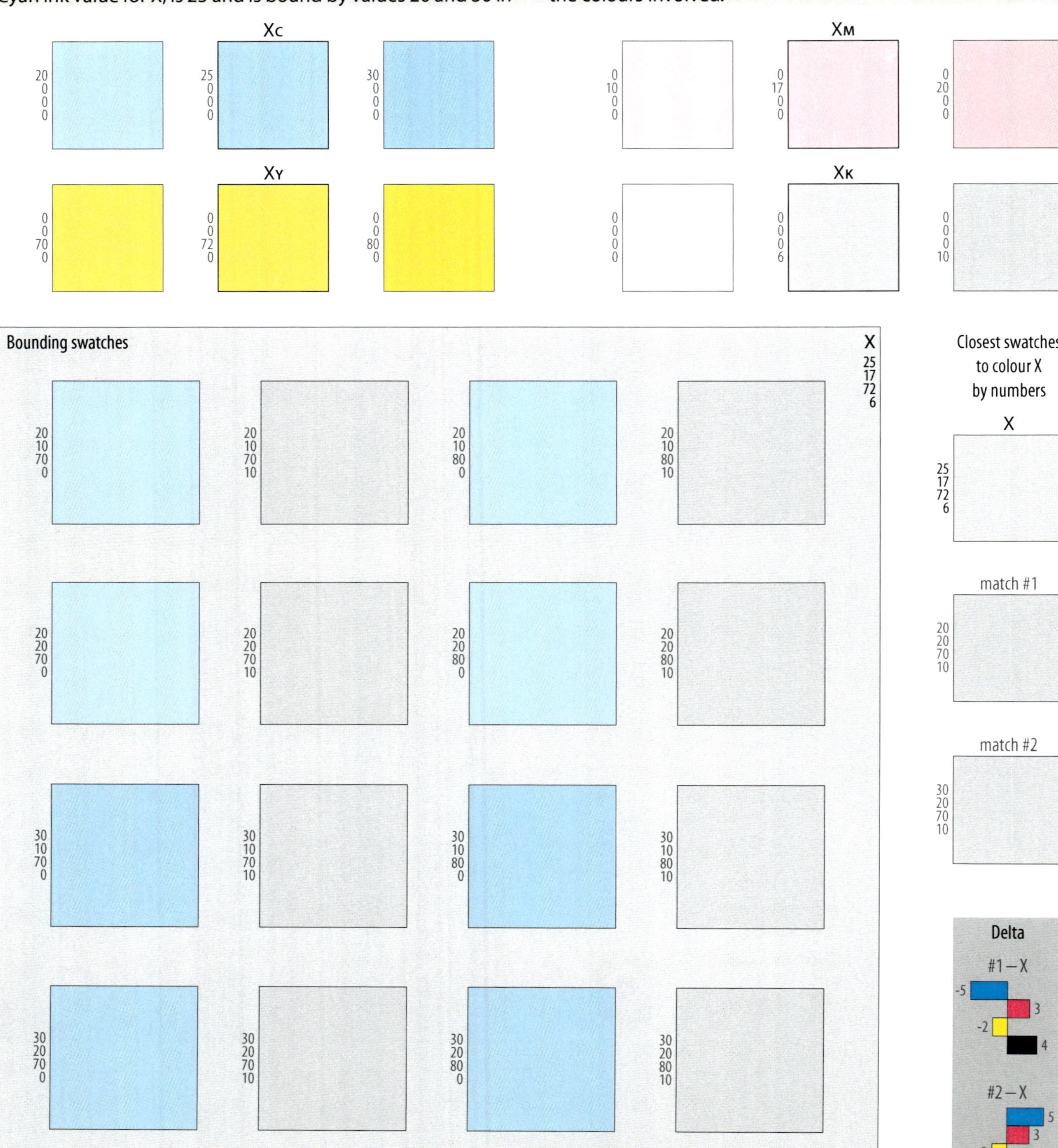

SEPARATIONS

MAP image plates

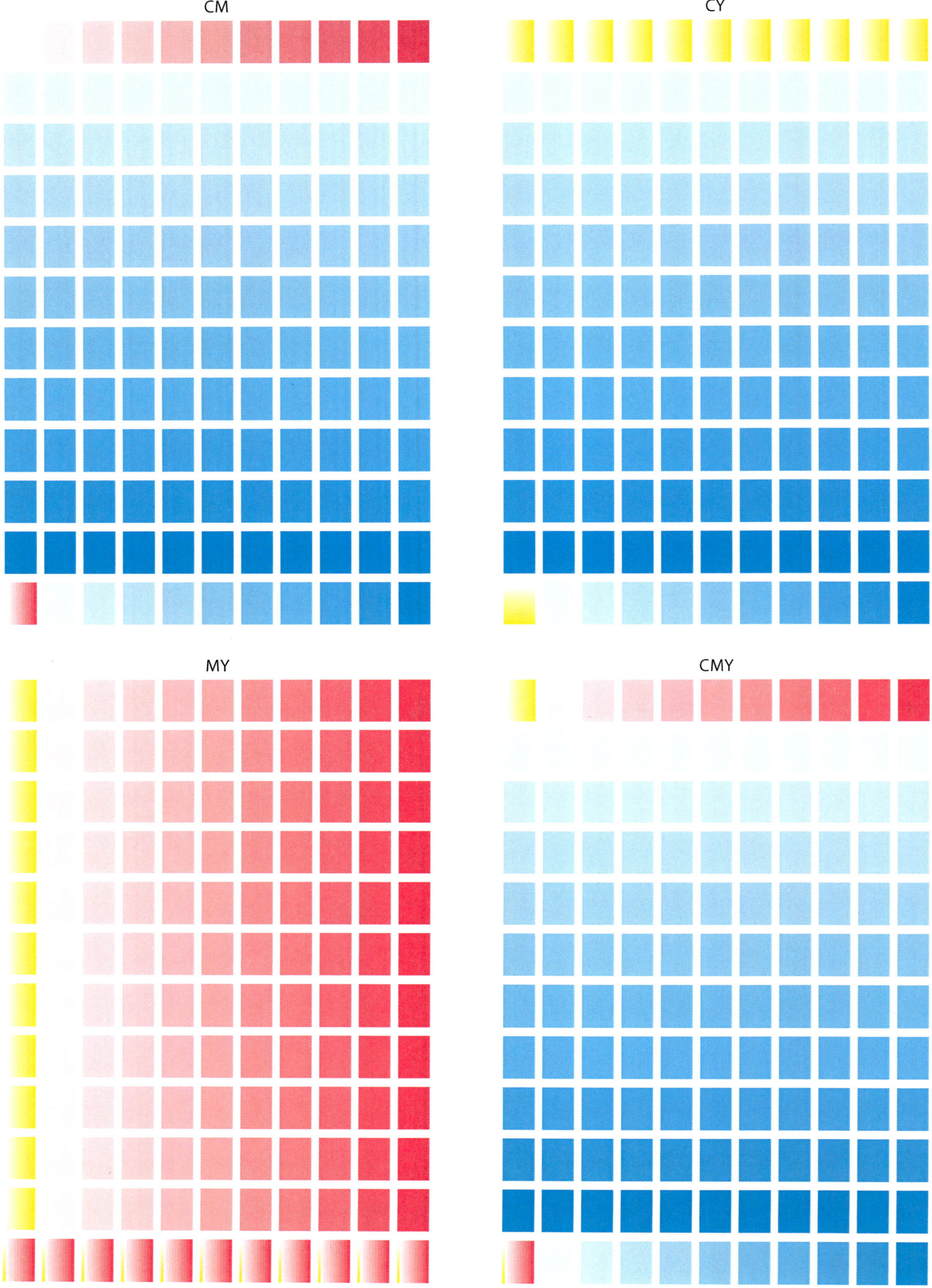
CM
CY
MY
CMY

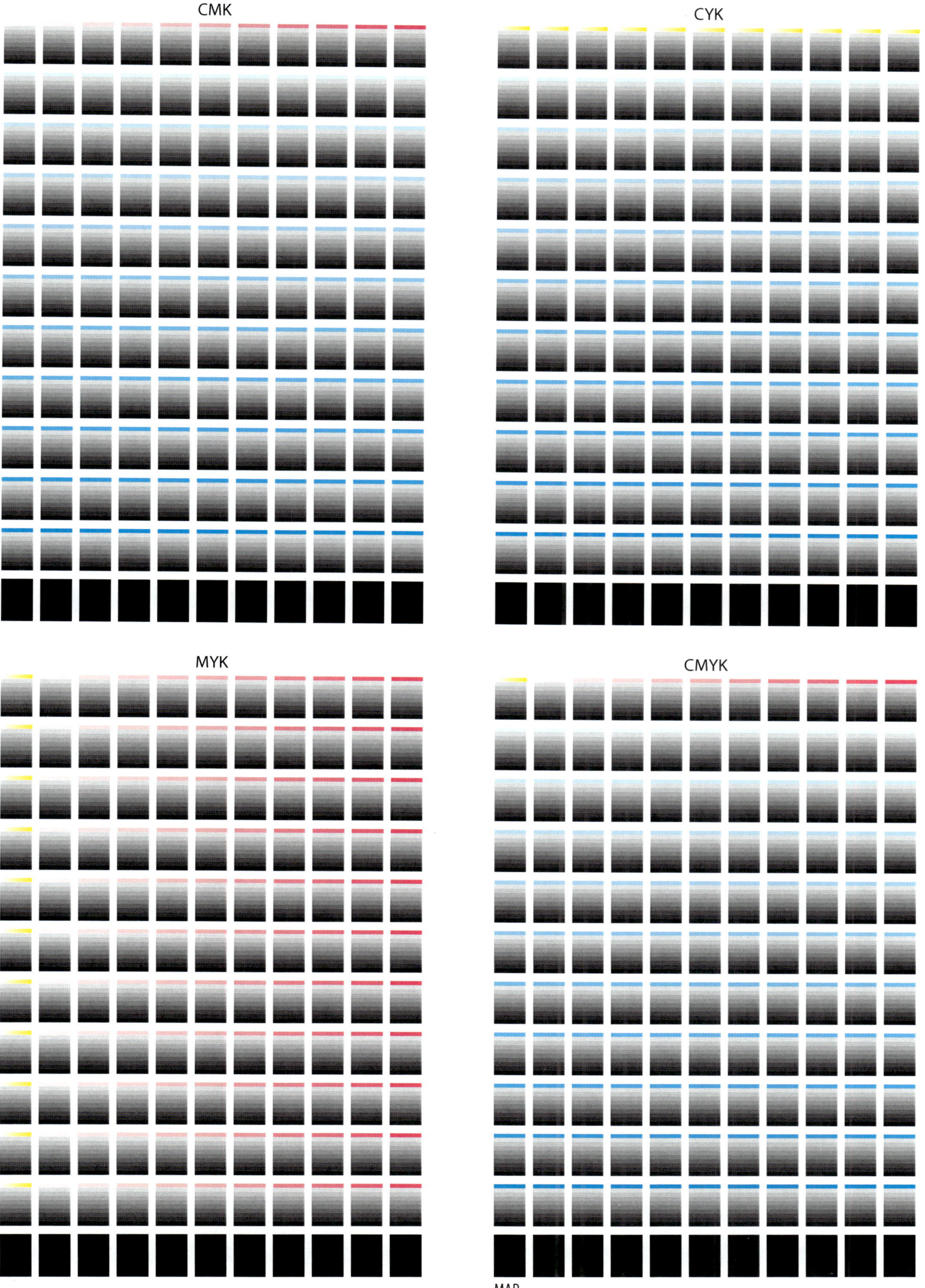
CMK
CYK
MYK
CMYK
MAP

0
10
20
30
40
50
60
70
80
90
100
0
10
20
30
40
50
60
70
80
90
K
Y
0C 0M

0
10
20
30
40
50
60
70
80
90
100
0
10
20
30
40
50
60
70
80
90
K
Y
0C 10M

0C 20M

0C 30M

0C 40M

0
10
20
30
40
50
60
70
80
90
100
0
10
20
30
40
50
60
70
80
90
K
Y
0C 50M

0
10
20
30
40
50
60
70
80
90
100
0
10
20
30
40
50
60
70
80
90
K
Y
0C 60M

0
10
20
30
40
50
60
70
80
90
100
0
10
20
30
40
50
60
70
80
90
K
0C 70M
Y

0
10
20
30
40
50
60
70
80
90
100
0
10
20
30
40
50
60
70
80
90
K
Y
0C 80M

0C 90M

0C 100M

10C 0M

10C 10M

10C 20M

10C 30M

10C 40M

10C 50M

10C 60M

	0	10	20	30	40	50	60	70	80	90	100
0											
10											
20											
30											
40											
50											
60											
70											
80											
90											

K

Y

10C 70M

10C 80M

10C 90M

10C 100M

20C 0M

20C 10M

0
10
20
30
40
50
60
70
80
90
100
0
10
20
30
40
50
60
70
80
90
K
Y
20C 20M

0 10 20 30 40 50 60 70 80 90 100
0
10
20
30
40
50
60
70
80
90
K
Y
20C 30M

20C 40M

20C 50M

	0	10	20	30	40	50	60	70	80	90	100
0											
10											
20											
30											
40											
50											
60											
70											
80											
90											

K

Y

20C 60M

20C 70M

0
10
20
30
40
50
60
70
80
90
100
0
10
20
30
40
50
60
70
80
90
K
Y
20C 80M

20C 90M

0
10
20
30
40
50
60
70
80
90
100
0
10
20
30
40
50
60
70
80
90
K
Y
20C 100M

0
10
20
30
40
50
60
70
80
90
100
0
10
20
30
40
50
60
70
80
90
K
Y
30C 0M

	0	10	20	30	40	50	60	70	80	90	100
0											
10											
20											
30											
40											
50											
60											
70											
80											
90											

K

Y

30C 10M

30C 20M

30C 30M

0 10 20 30 40 50 60 70 80 90 100
0
10
20
30
40
50
60
70
80
90
K
Y
30C 40M

30C 50M

30C 60M

30C 70M

30C 80M

30C 90M

30C 100M

40C 0M

40C 10M

40C 20M

40C 30M

40C 40M

0
10
20
30
40
50
60
70
80
90
100
0
10
20
30
40
50
60
70
80
90
K
Y
40C 50M

40C 60M

0
10
20
30
40
50
60
70
80
90
100
0
10
20
30
40
50
60
70
80
90
K
Y
40C 70M

K \ Y	0	10	20	30	40	50	60	70	80	90	100
0											
10											
20											
30											
40											
50											
60											
70											
80											
90											

K

Y

40C 80M

40C 90M

0
10
20
30
40
50
60
70
80
90
100
0
10
20
30
40
50
60
70
80
90
K
Y
40C 100M

0
10
20
30
40
50
60
70
80
90
100
0
10
20
30
40
50
60
70
80
90
K
Y
50C 0M

50C 10M

0
10
20
30
40
50
60
70
80
90
100
0
10
20
30
40
50
60
70
80
90
K
Y
50C 20M

50C 30M

50C 40M

50C 50M

50C 60M

50C 70M

50C 80M

50C 90M

50C 100M

0
10
20
30
40
50
60
70
80
90
100
0
10
20
30
40
50
60
70
80
90
K
Y
60C 0M

60C 10M

60C 20M

60C 30M

60C 40M

60C 50M

60C 60M

0 10 20 30 40 50 60 70 80 90 100
0
10
20
30
40
50
60
70
80
90
K
Y
60C 70M

60C 80M

60C 90M

60C 100M

70C 0M

70C 10M

0 10 20 30 40 50 60 70 80 90 100
0
10
20
30
40
50
60
70
80
90
K
Y
70C 20M

70C 30M

0
10
20
30
40
50
60
70
80
90
100
0
10
20
30
40
50
60
70
80
90
K
Y
70C 40M

70C 50M

70C 60M

0 10 20 30 40 50 60 70 80 90 100
0
10
20
30
40
50
60
70
80
90
K
Y
70C 70M

70C 80M

70C 90M

0
10
20
30
40
50
60
70
80
90
100
0
10
20
30
40
50
60
70
80
90
K
Y
70C 100M

0 10 20 30 40 50 60 70 80 90 100
0
10
20
30
40
50
60
70
80
90
K
Y
80C 0M

80C 10M

80C 20M

0
10
20
30
40
50
60
70
80
90
100
0
10
20
30
40
50
60
70
80
90
K
Y
80C 30M

80C 40M

80C 50M

0
10
20
30
40
50
60
70
80
90
100
0
10
20
30
40
50
60
70
80
90
K
Y
80C 60M

80C 70M

0
10
20
30
40
50
60
70
80
90
100
0
10
20
30
40
50
60
70
80
90
K
Y
80C 80M

80C 90M

80C 100M

0
10
20
30
40
50
60
70
80
90
100
0
10
20
30
40
50
60
70
80
90
K
Y
90C 0M

90C 10M

90C 20M

90C 30M

90C 40M

0
10
20
30
40
50
60
70
80
90
100
0
10
20
30
40
50
60
70
80
90
K
Y
90C 50M

0
10
20
30
40
50
60
70
80
90
100
0
10
20
30
40
50
60
70
80
90
K
Y
90C 60M

0
10
20
30
40
50
60
70
80
90
100
0
10
20
30
40
50
60
70
80
90
K
Y
90C 70M

90C 80M

90C 90M

0
10
20
30
40
50
60
70
80
90
100
0
10
20
30
40
50
60
70
80
90
K
Y
90C 100M

0
10
20
30
40
50
60
70
80
90
100
0
10
20
30
40
50
60
70
80
90
K
Y
100C 0M

0
10
20
30
40
50
60
70
80
90
100
0
10
20
30
40
50
60
70
80
90
K
Y
100C 10M

100C 20M

100C 30M

0
10
20
30
40
50
60
70
80
90
100
0
10
20
30
40
50
60
70
80
90
K
Y
100C 40M

100C 50M

100C 60M

100C 70M

100C 80M

100C 90M

0
10
20
30
40
50
60
70
80
90
100
0
10
20
30
40
50
60
70
80
90
K
Y
100C 100M

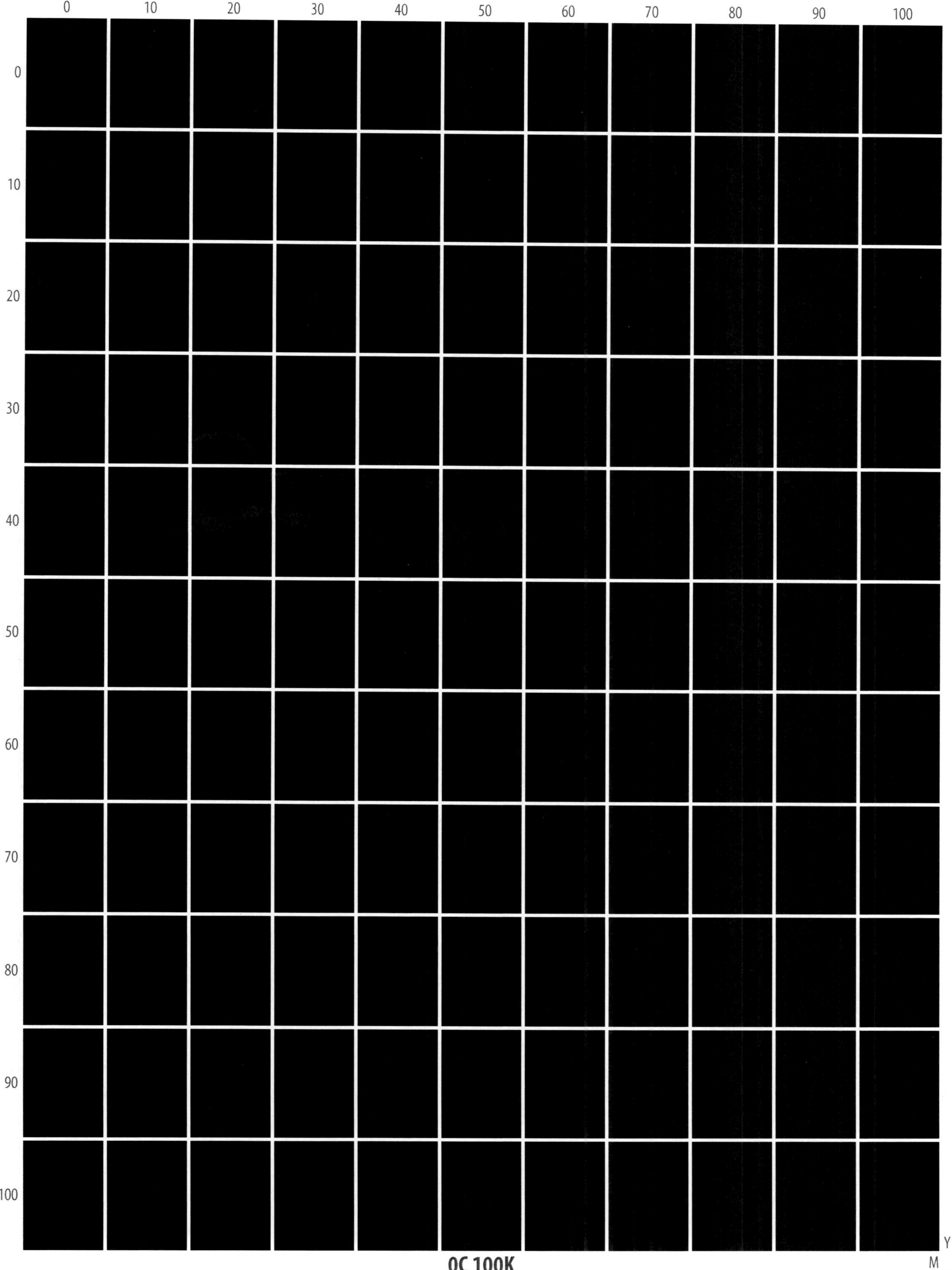

0C 100K

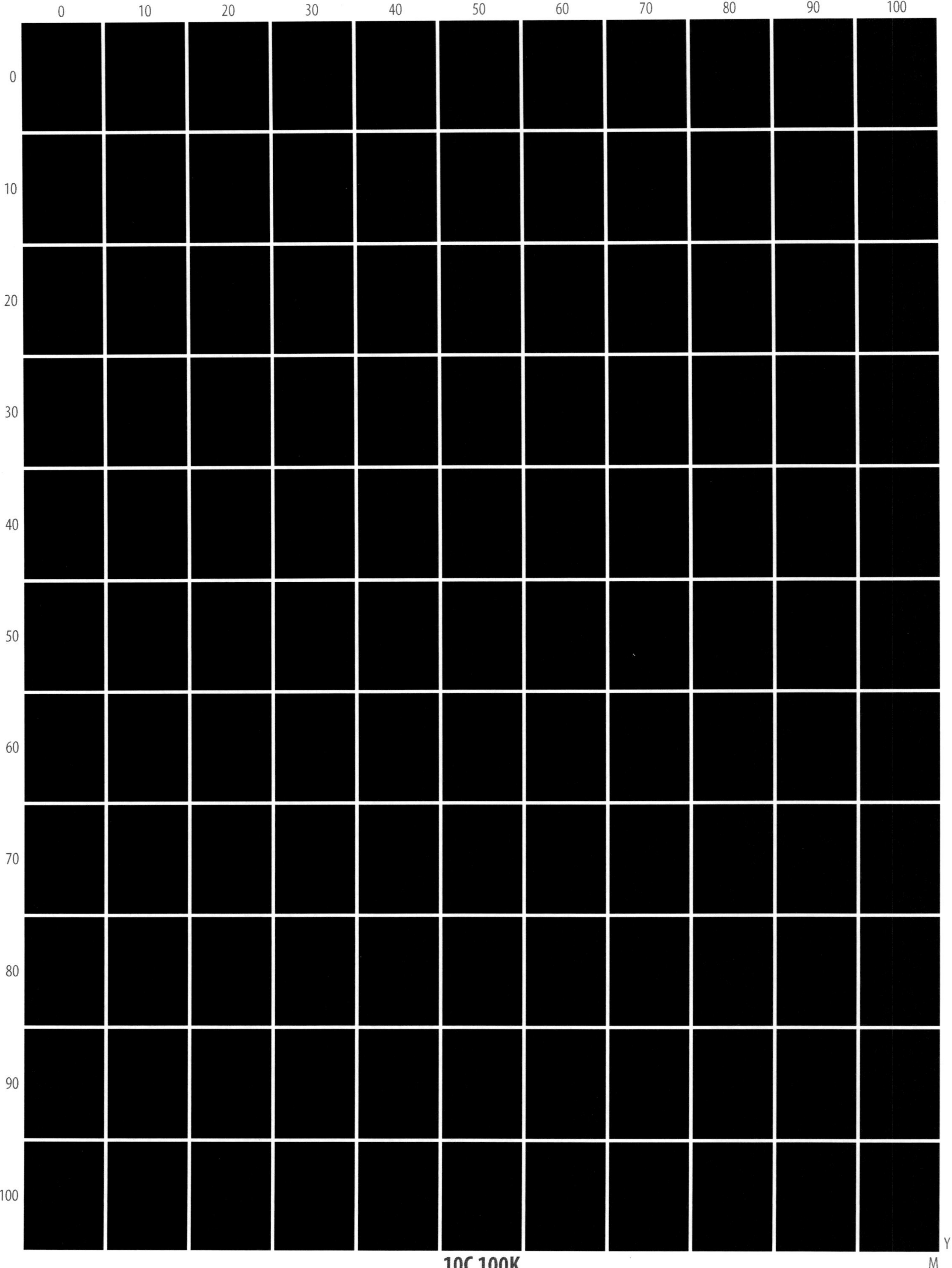

10C 100K

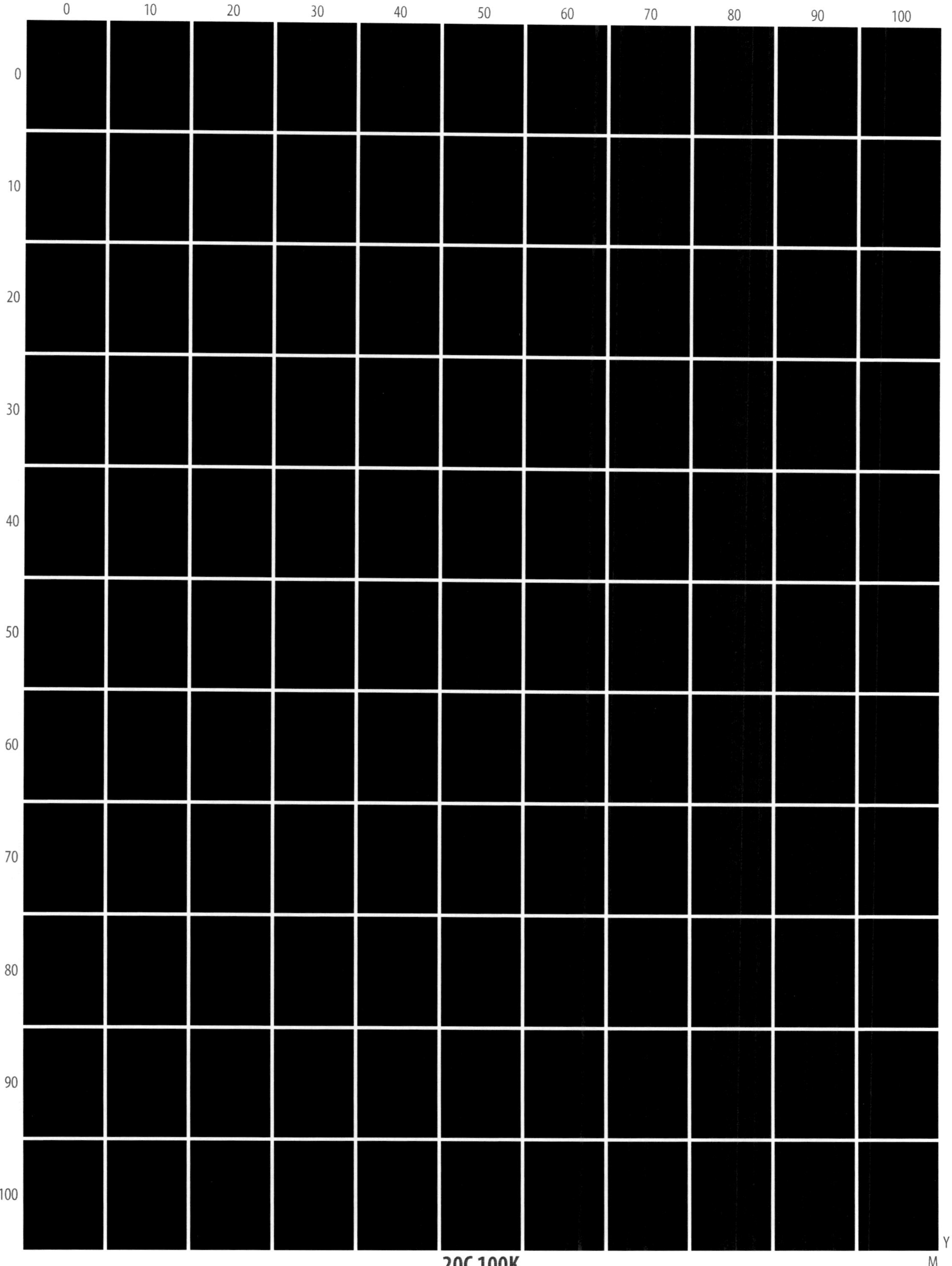

20C 100K

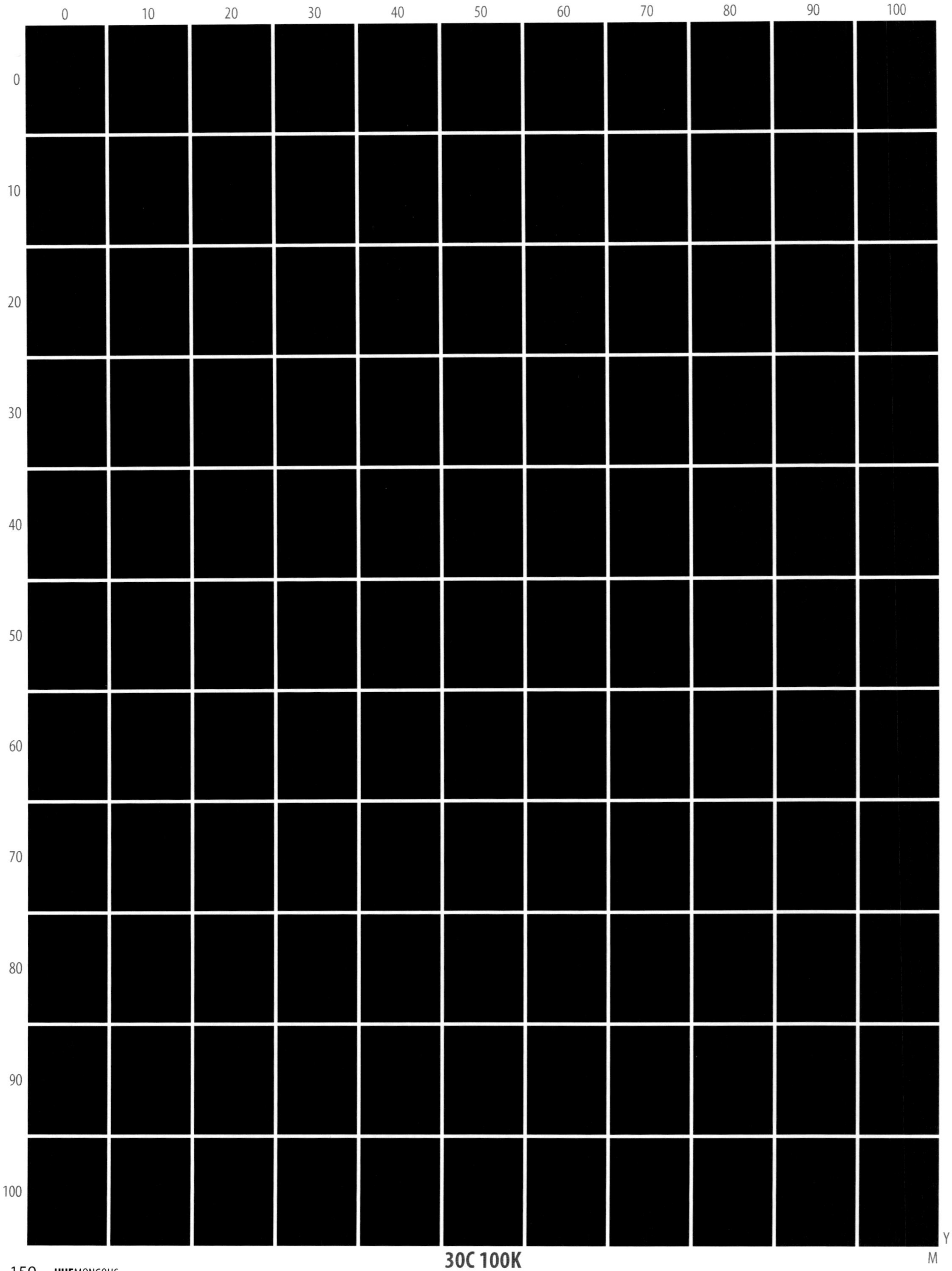

30C 100K

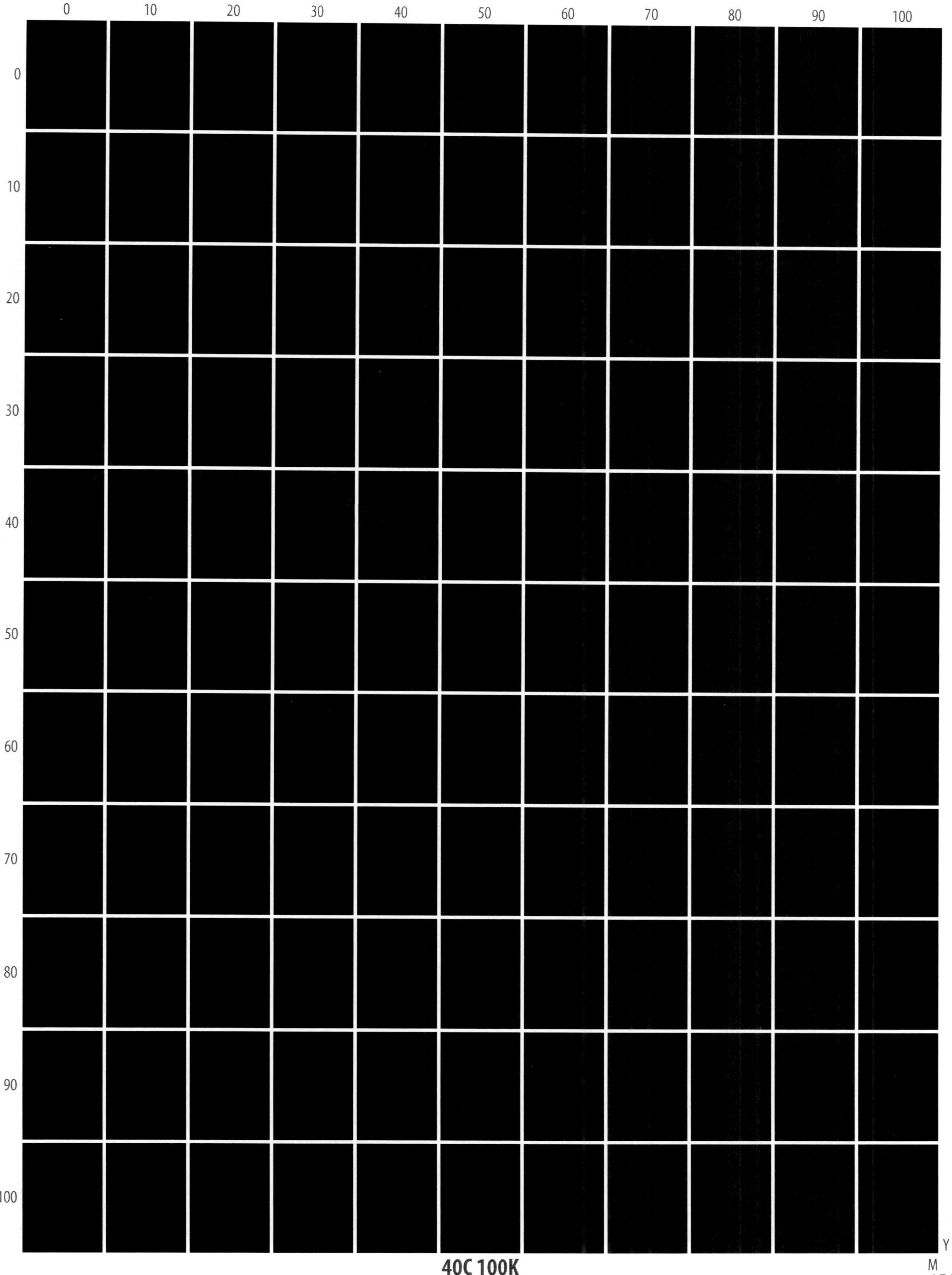

40C 100K

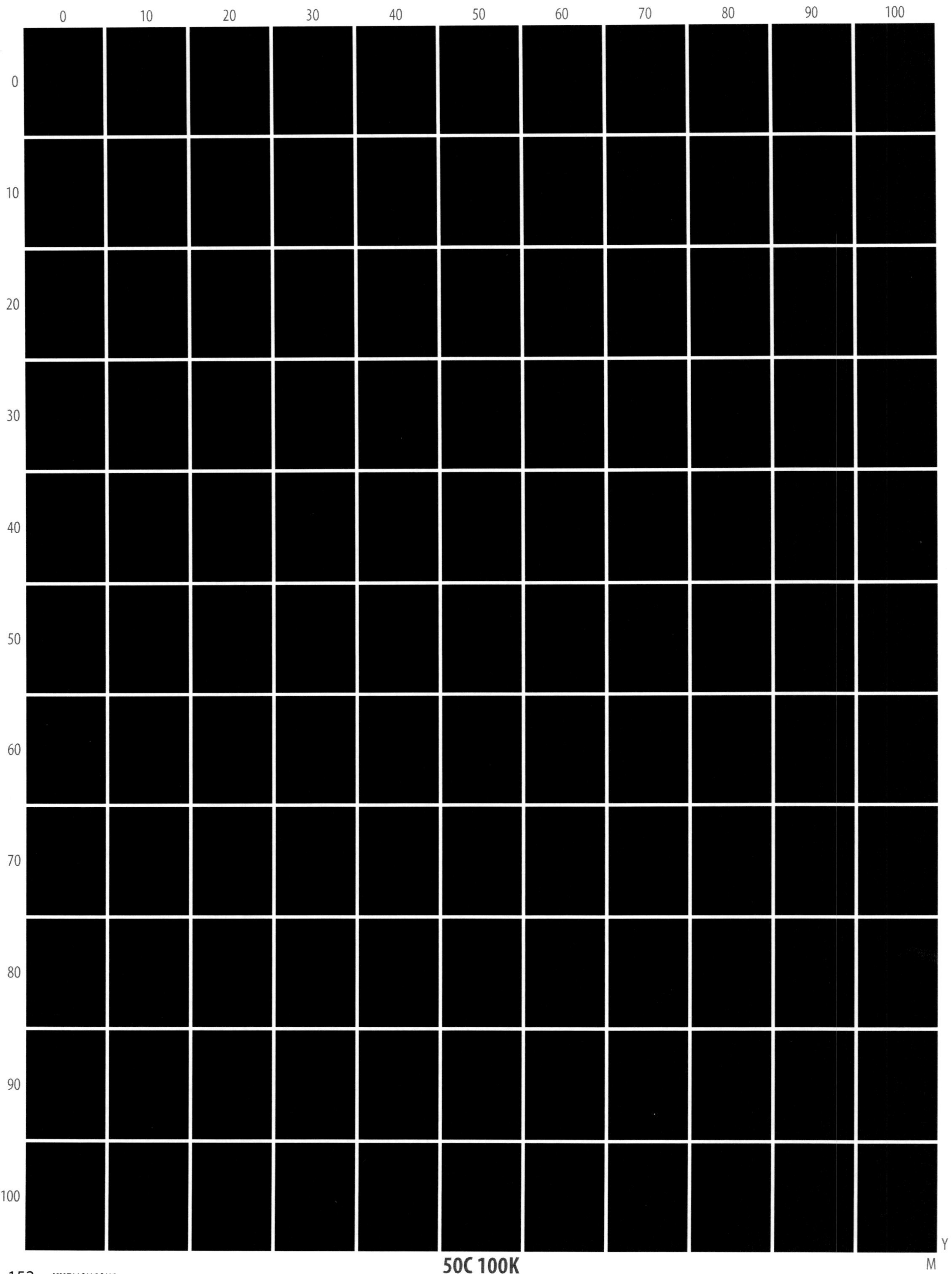

50C 100K

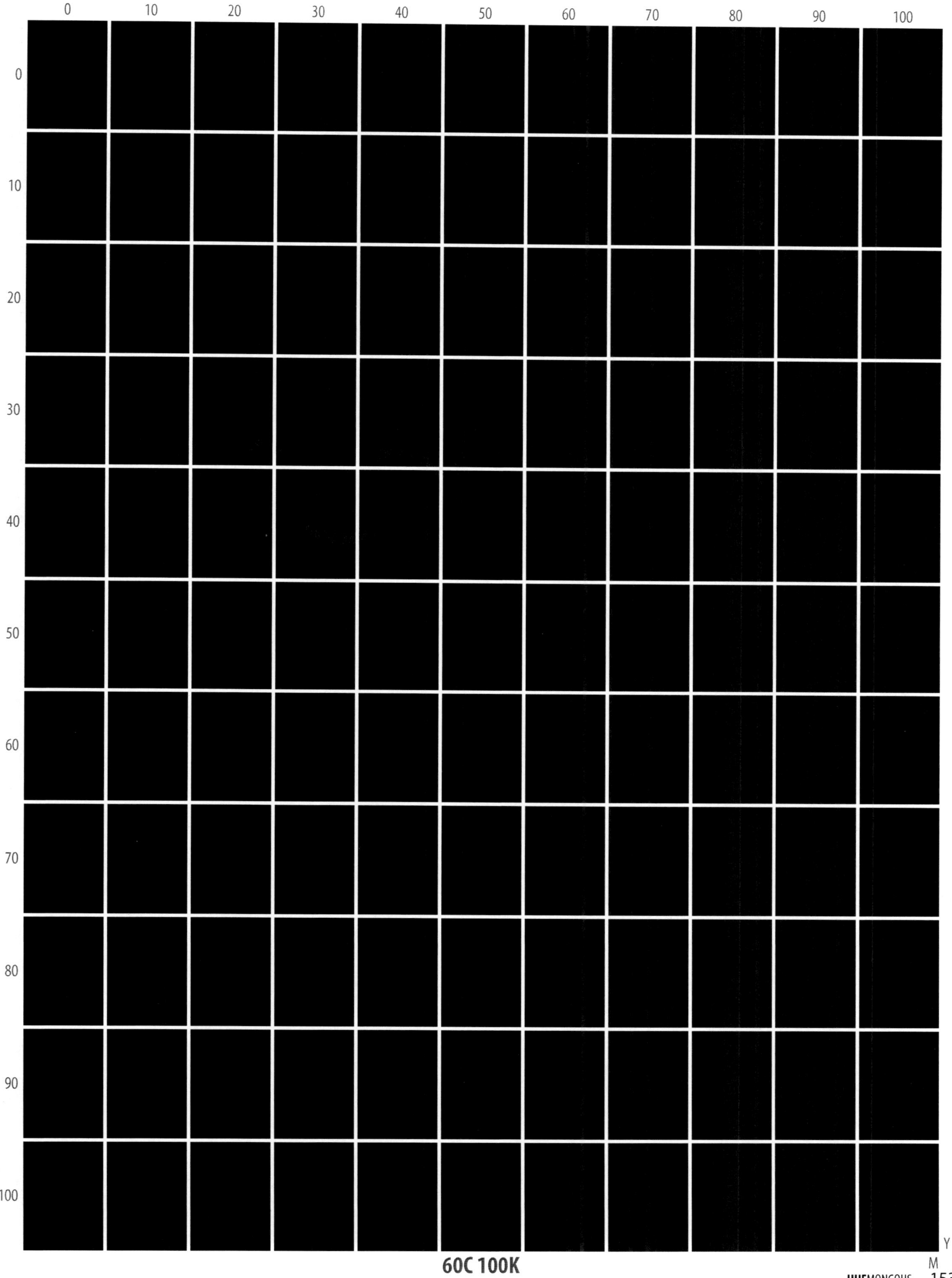

60C 100K

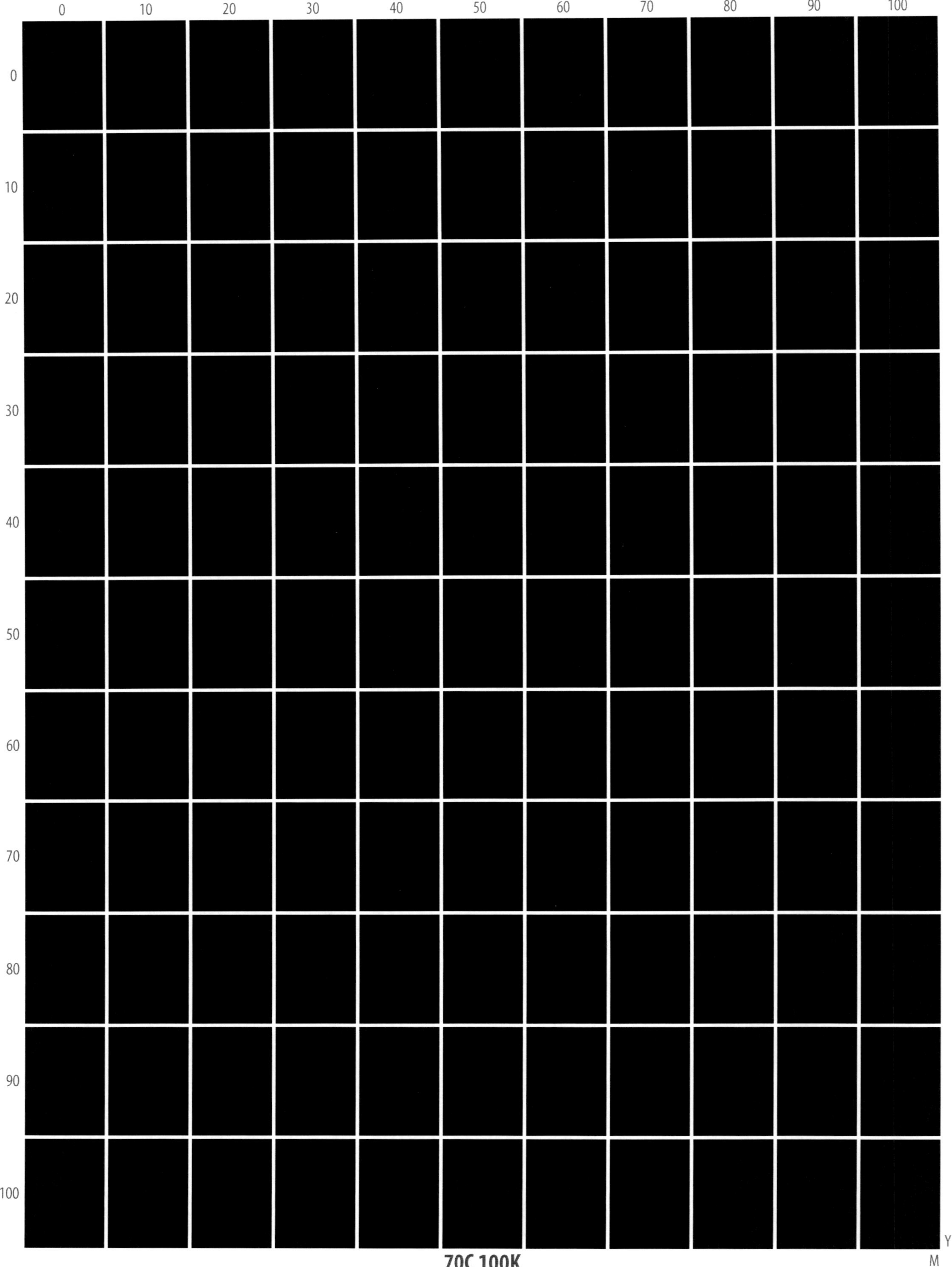

70C 100K

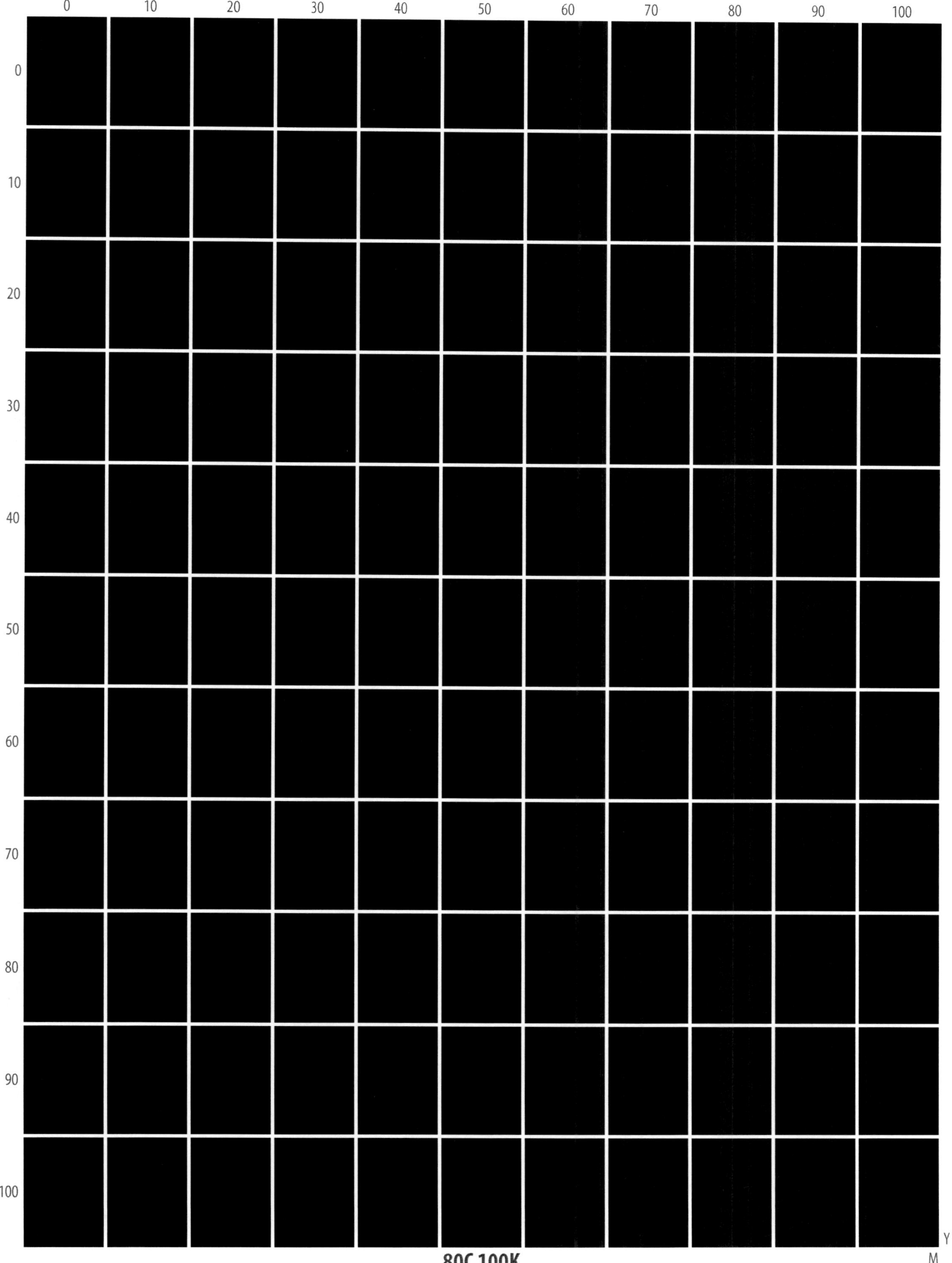
0 10 20 30 40 50 60 70 80 90 100
0 10 20 30 40 50 60 70 80 90 100
Y
M
80C 100K

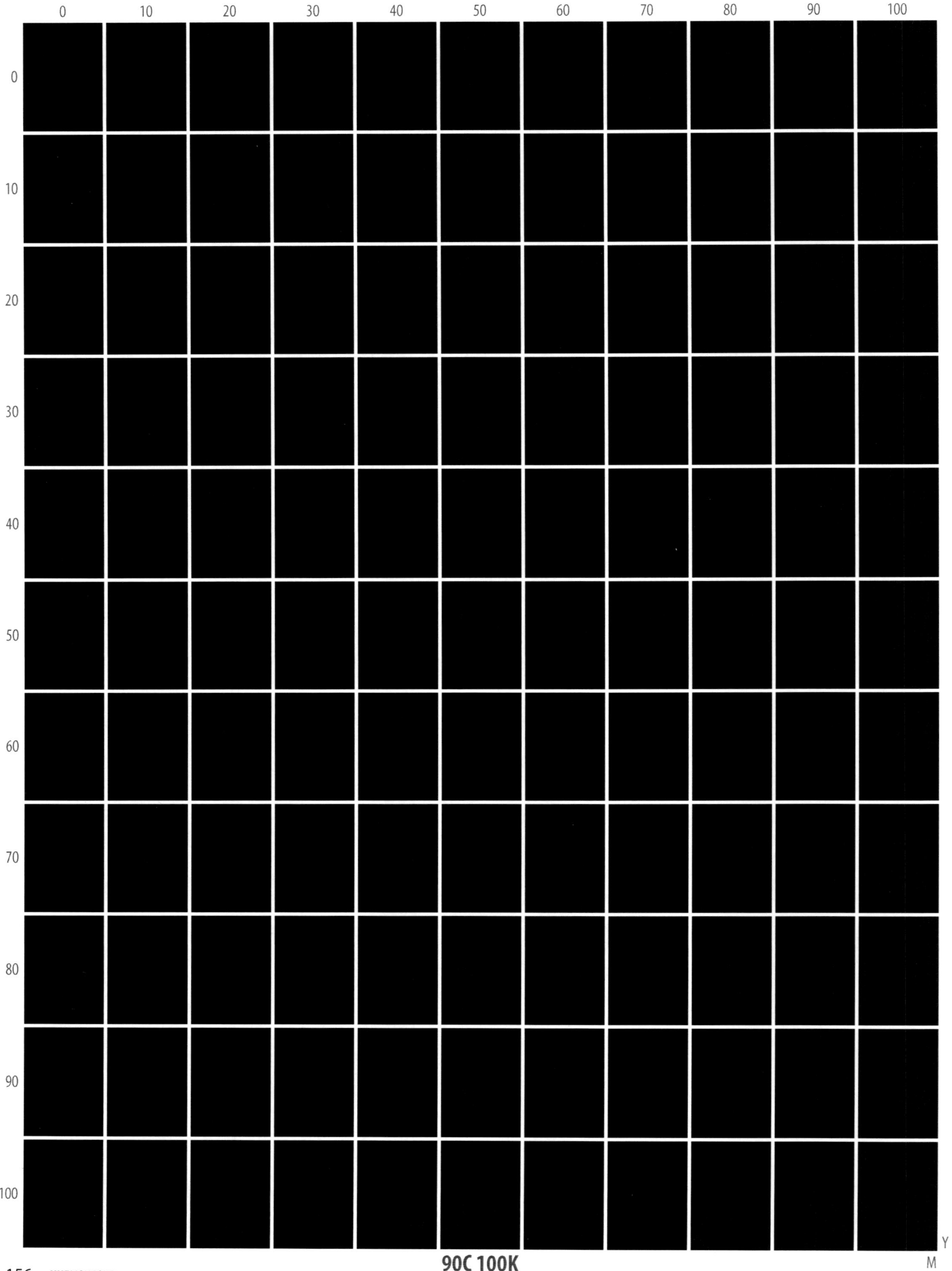

90C 100K

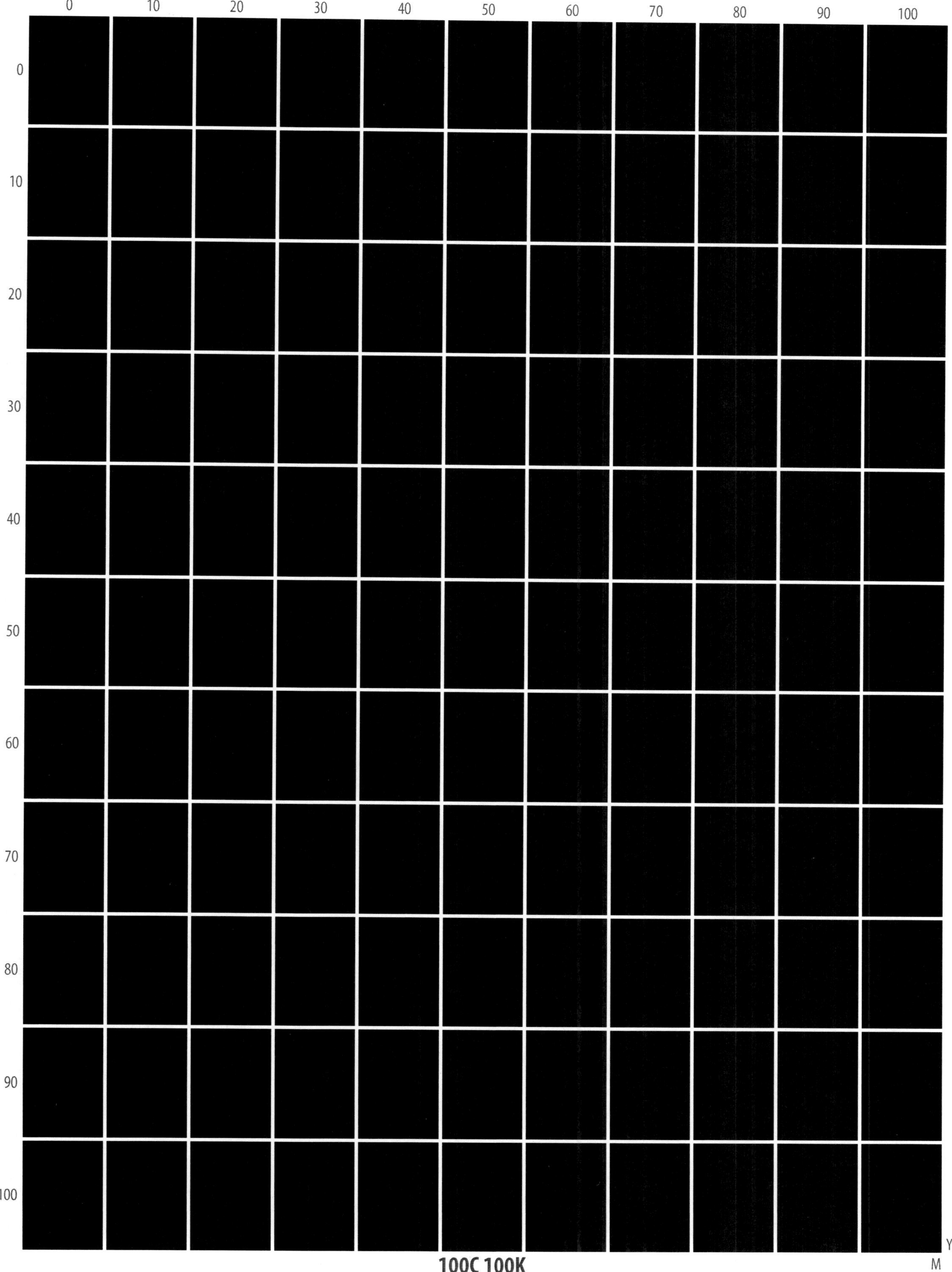

100C 100K

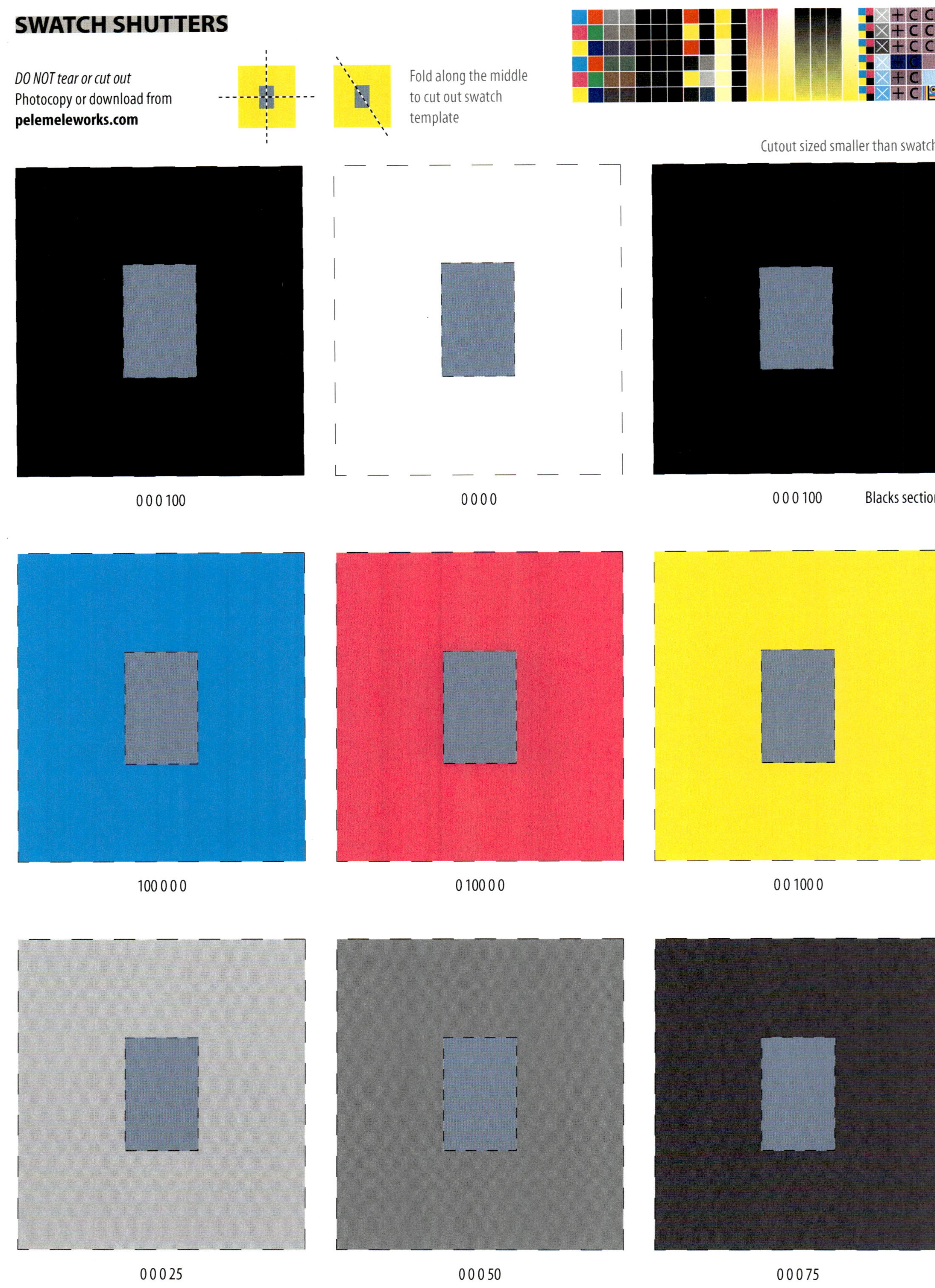
SWATCH SHUTTERS
DO NOT tear or cut out
Photocopy or download from
pelemeleworks.com
Fold along the middle
to cut out swatch
template
Cutout sized smaller than swatch
0 0 0 100
0 0 0 0
0 0 0 100
Blacks section
100 0 0 0
0 100 0 0
0 0 100 0
0 0 0 25
0 0 0 50
0 0 0 75

[**pelemeleworks.**com]

Questions? Suggestions? **Get in touch** through the website.

Stay informed of updates, promotions, and new releases. **Subscribe to the mailing list**.

Support Pêle-Mêle Works titles. **Write a review** on Amazon or elsewhere.

Thank you.

Made in the USA
Las Vegas, NV
05 March 2021